# BUSINESS SUCCESS FROM SEIZING THE ENVIRONMENTAL INITIATIVE

# BUSINESS SUCCESS FROM SEIZING THE ENVIRONMENTAL INITIATIVE

**Christine Hemming,**
***Chrisalis Environmental Consulting***

BUSINESS AND THE ENVIRONMENT PRACTITIONER SERIES
SERIES EDITOR: RUTH HILLARY
CENTRE FOR ENVIRONMENTAL TECHNOLOGY
IMPERIAL COLLEGE OF SCIENCE, TECHNOLOGY
AND MEDICINE

Published by:
TECHNICAL COMMUNICATIONS (PUBLISHING) LTD.

ISBN 0 946655 93 6



100 High Avenue
Letchworth
Hertfordshire SG6 3RR
England

Telephone/Fax: (0462) 679987



Printed by Information Press Ltd., Oxford, England

# CONTENTS

**ACKNOWLEDGEMENTS**

The case studies presented in this report are based on successful entries to an environmental award scheme, known as the PA Golden Leaf Awards, organised by PA Consulting Group with the help of the Conservation Foundation. Successful entries were those which best demonstrated benefits to the environment together with lasting business advantage to the company.

The case studies have been selected to illustrate some of the ways in which successful businesses can be built upon a positive approach to environmental pressures. The award winners include many more, equally impressive, examples. I am grateful to PA for the opportunity and privilege of managing the PA Golden Leaf Awards while I was working for the company. Nevertheless, the opinions given in this report are mine alone, and I have been asked to make it clear that PA has not participated in the report's publication.

I am also grateful to the companies featured here for allowing me to use them as examples and for their help in preparing the case studies.

## PREFACE

In 1987, the World Commission on Environment and Development (the Brundtland Commission) published a report entitled 'Our Common Future'. This report first established the concept of 'sustainable development', which was defined as meaning continued development to meet the needs of the present without compromising the ability of future generations to meet their own needs. The report marked the beginning of the reemergence of environmental issues at the top of the political agenda and the end of the idea that economic progress and protection of the environment are mutually exclusive goals. Two years later, environmental parties achieved unprecedented success in European Parliament elections and Mrs Thatcher, then Prime Minister, was talking of 'no inconsistency between economic growth and environmental protection'.

Some companies have been aware for many years that 'Pollution Prevention Pays', as 3M puts it. Yet within the majority of businesses, environmental pressures continue to mean only increased expenditure and increased costs. A survey carried out by PA Consulting Group for the Confederation of British Industry in 1990 found that most companies regarded environmental issues as an unmitigated burden, and little has changed since. Indeed, the recession has prompted a change in priorities, and made many companies even less likely to spend more than the minimum necessary on the environment.

It was to counter this generally negative view that PA established the Golden Leaf Awards in 1990. The aim was to draw attention to companies which had been able successfully to meet environmental and business objectives at the same time. This book draws on some of the award winners to provide examples of the many ways in which companies can achieve business success with a positive approach to environmental pressures, and thereby put the principle of sustainable development into practice at the business level.

## ABOUT THE AUTHOR

Dr Christine Hemming has recently started her own environmental consultancy business. Its focus is on helping clients develop a positive approach to environmental pressures, based on integrating a scientific understanding of the environmental impacts and risks into a practical management response.

Dr Hemming has a B.Sc. in mathematics and physics and a D.Phil. in theoretical physics. Her working career began at the National Radiological Protection Board, developing computer models of the fate of radioactivity released into the environment, and she has worked in the general field of environmental protection ever since. Six years with NRPB were followed by five years with the Department of the Environment working in the fields of radioactive waste management, air quality and environmental protection technologies.

Dr Hemming left the DoE in 1990 to join PA Consulting Group to help develop PA's environmental consultancy business. During her time with PA, she managed the PA Golden Leaf Awards, an annual award scheme established by PA and the Conservation Foundation to recognise companies which have combined environmental improvement with business success. She was Assignment Manager of the studies PA carried out for the British Government to develop criteria for the award of eco-labels for washing machines and dishwashers under a new European Community scheme. She also managed a pilot exercise for the European Commission on the implementation of a new EC Regulation on eco-management and audit.

Dr Hemming has spoken at many conferences and seminars on the practical application of life cycle assessment techniques, and is now an acknowledged expert in this field. She has also spoken at seminars and published articles on environmental management systems and the EC eco-management and audit scheme.

Contact details are as follows:

Chrisalis Environmental Consulting
8 South View
Stortford Road
Great Dunmow
Essex, CM6 1UQ

Telephone: 0371 872547
Facsimile: 0371 872547

# Chapter 1

# INTRODUCTION

The growth in environmental concern is still widely regarded as threatening by many businesses. In the UK this is partly attributable to recent legislative pressure in the form of EC Directives and the 1990 Environmental Protection Act, and more recent concerns about liabilities for the cost of cleaning up historic contamination. The general perception is that higher environmental standards mean an increased burden on businesses and merely increase their costs.

However, as with any pressure for change, environmental pressures also offer opportunities for far-sighted businesses. Waste is a sign of inefficiency, and cost reductions are an inevitable benefit of energy saving or waste minimisation programmes. There is an awareness amongst consumers about the environmental effects of products and companies can use this awareness to increase market share, especially if the environmentally better products are also competitive on cost and quality grounds. Legislators rarely take enough account of the specific planning timetables of individual businesses when bringing in new environmental laws. The company which has established its own continual improvement programme will be able to keep ahead of legislation and manage its capital expenditure programme according to its *own* priorities rather than those of the regulator.

The more environmentally aware companies have recognised this for some time and have gained competitive advantage as a result. Some of the better known examples include 3M which has had a 'Pollution Prevention Pays' (or '3P') programme since 1975. The company estimates that this programme has saved more than $500 million over the years by eliminating or reducing capital expenditure and operating costs. Other examples are highlighted in an Executive Guide prepared by Business in the Environment.

However, these examples are more generally found amongst the larger companies. The companies which most need to be made aware of the threats and opportunities which environmental pressures will generate are the small- to medium-sized companies. At present they are likely to feel that their first priorities lie elsewhere, but these companies will be coming under increasing pressure in the future, not only from legislation but also from their customers. The larger companies which have established an environmental policy and action programme have usually identified the environmental performance of their suppliers as an important issue. Some have already written to their suppliers to ask about their environmental policies. The introduction of the British Standard on Environmental Management Systems, BS7750, and of the European Community Regulation on eco-management and audit has provided a ready-made framework on which companies can base requirements for their suppliers, in much the same way that the Quality Management Systems standard, BS5750,

has been used as a basis for quality requirements.

The aim of this report is to describe some of the ways in which UK businesses, from the large to the very small, have been able to improve their environmental performance and their business performance at the same time. A number of general themes are explored and then illustrated with short case study examples. The examples have all been taken from successful entries to an environmental award scheme organised by PA Consulting Group and the Conservation Foundation. The aim of this scheme was to find the best examples of companies which had created business advantage from an environmentally responsible approach. Successful entries included sensitive restorations of quarries, improved management systems, waste recovery, reuse and recycling programmes, energy saving systems, and cleaner technologies.

On the basis that the best way to describe how to do something is to give an example, this book aims to show how to combine business success and a better environment by describing how other companies have managed to achieve this. It is intended for the business manager with a general understanding of the issues and concepts, and for the environmental manager who would find some concrete examples useful in persuading his/her chief executive that responding to environmental pressures need not just represent a deduction from profits.

# Chapter 2

# RECOGNISING THE TRENDS

## Environmental Pressures on Business

The existence of environmental pressures continues to be an important issue for business and these pressures are affecting a growing number of industries. The issue has seemed to drop down the political agenda a little in the last few years, largely as a result of the recession, when other issues such as unemployment assume priority, but it is certain to resurface. The simple reason for this is that the Earth's resources are finite and they are currently being used at a faster rate than they are being replenished. This situation is not sustainable and will need to be addressed.

There is uncertainty over the current scientific evidence for global warming and of the dangers of the hole in the ozone layer. It is possible to conceive that man's ingenuity will be able to solve the problems which may arise by technological fixes. And it can be difficult to comprehend how global problems can be solved by individual action. However, these questions are largely irrelevant for most businesses. What matters for them is that these global issues, (and others which may be more specific to different countries or different regions within countries) create concern within groups which have an influence on a company's operations, and these concerns need to be addressed if the company is to continue operating successfully. The situation is illustrated in Figure 2.1.

The general public has a certain level of environmental awareness and concern as a result of a large number of influences, including culture, history, geography, education and economics. This level of awareness and concern can be heightened by the activities of pressure groups and by reporting in the media. It is public pressure more than any other source which influences changes in legislation, although pressure groups and other interest groups can have a direct influence on the development of legislation. Other influencers include international pressures and commitments, such as the UK's membership of the European Community or the United Nations.

Businesses need to comply with the law and therefore are subject to pressures from legislative changes. They can influence the development of new legislation, but to do so need to be aware of how legislation is developed both within the UK and internationally. Particularly important in this context is the European Community which is increasingly setting the agenda for environmental legislation in the UK.

Businesses are also subject to other pressures. They wish to sell to customers and eventually, at the end of the supply chain, these customers are the general

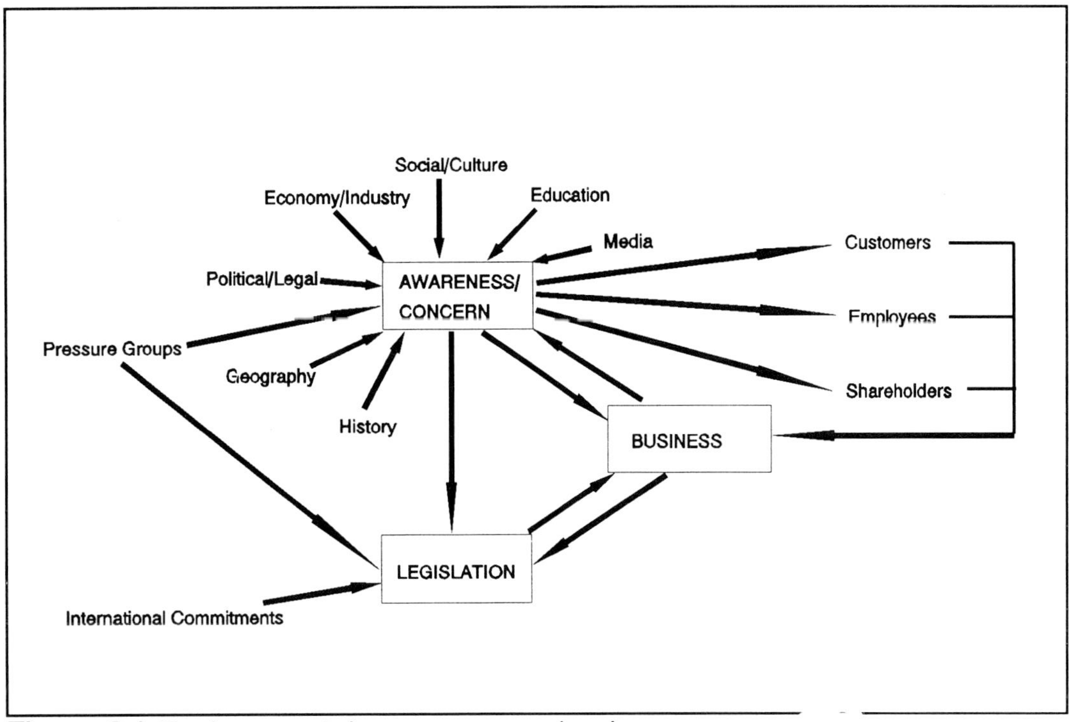


**Figure 2.1** Environmental pressures on business

public whose awareness and concern can manifest themselves in purchasing decisions. Although the consumer who chooses the environmentally least damaging product irrespective of other factors may never have been a significant force in the marketplace, environmental issues remain one factor among the many that consumers take account of in their choices, and the environmental aspects of goods remain a feature of the advertising of a large number of products from washing detergents to cars.

A company's employees are crucial to its business. The recession has again shifted the supply and demand balance in favour of the employer, but in the longer term the ageing of the population will increase competition amongst employers to recruit and retain the best people. A factor which these people will consider in choosing an employer will be the company's record on the environment. A company which has a positive programme of environmental improvement will find it easier to recruit the best people, and it will also find that such a programme can help to improve staff motivation and job satisfaction.

A company's shareholders have an important influence on the way it operates. With increasing share ownership, the views of these shareholders increasingly reflect those of the general public, with greater emphasis on broader issues such as the impact of the company's operations on the environment. In addition, with greater awareness of the scale of potential environmental liabilities, shareholders wish to be assured that companies are doing everything they can to minimise these. There is also increasing evidence that companies with a good

environmental record perform better. The company's bank and insurance company will similarly be concerned about the potential liability for environmental cleanup costs.

More and more companies are becoming exposed to these pressures. Whereas in the 1960s and 1970s, it was mainly industries such as the nuclear industry, the chemical industry, and mining and quarrying which found themselves under pressure, in the 1990s even a company such as British Telecom feels the need to produce an annual report on its environmental performance.

## International Issues

Nor is it any longer the case that increasing environmental pressures in one location can be circumvented by moving elsewhere. Environmental standards are increasingly set on an international basis. The European Community treaties provide a means for harmonising environmental standards across Europe. The Earth Summit in Rio de Janeiro in June 1992 heightened worldwide awareness of the problems of environmental degradation, and the conventions signed there provide a mechanism for promulgating equivalent environmental standards in all countries. Different environmental standards are perceived as being unfair to trade and are therefore likely to be short-lived.

Research carried out by PA Consulting Group has looked at the levels of environmental awareness and of environmental performance achieved in 13 developed countries around the world. The results of this research indicated that the countries could be divided into roughly three groups in terms of the levels of awareness and of environmental performance, as shown in Figure 2.2.

The trend is for harmonisation of performance standards as laid down in legislation and therefore for all countries to move towards the top right hand corner of the diagram.

The picture is therefore clear: no business can afford to ignore the environment; no industry sector is immune; no country in the world is immune.

## Perceptions Versus the 'Facts'

A further characteristic of environmental pressures which needs to be recognised is that, in this field, perceptions about issues are at least as important as, and often more important than, the facts. This can again be illustrated by reference to research carried out by PA into the issue of packaging.

Firstly, the facts: packaging waste accounts for about 25% of the total municipal solid waste generated in the UK, which in turn makes up only 4% of all solid

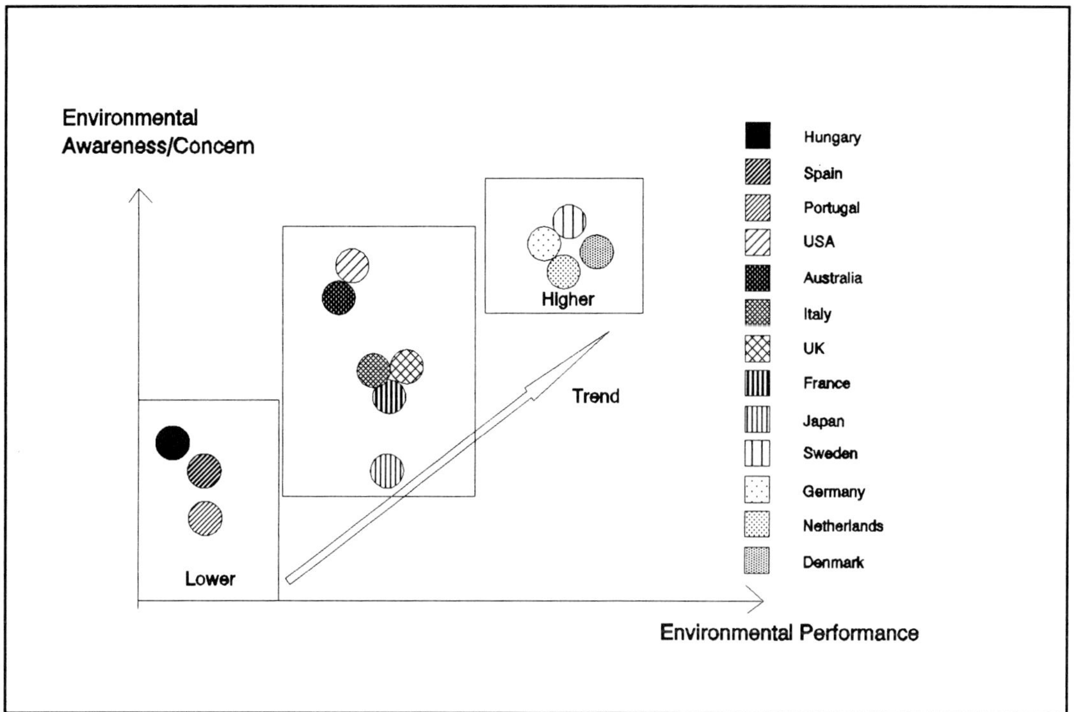


**Figure 2.2** International trends

waste produced (the remainder being agricultural, mining, construction and industrial). It therefore represents a very minor component of the country's solid waste disposal problem. Packaging, particularly of food products, is good for the environment in that it protects goods from damage or contamination and thus reduces wastage. Figure 2.3 compares the average food spoilage rates in developed and less developed countries and shows the beneficial effects of packaging.

Yet despite this picture, packaging waste is a major target for environmental legislation. Germany introduced the concept of making the producer of a product responsible for its ultimate disposal, and chose packaging as the first product to which this concept applied. The law in Germany gave consumers the right to return packaging to the point of sale and led to the establishment of the Duales System Deutschlands (DSD) and the 'green dot' to be seen on packaging in Germany. As well as sorting problems, this scheme has resulted in the collection of mountains of recovered packaging material for which there is no market. The value of recovered paper and plastics has plummeted across the whole of Europe, and this has seriously disrupted the economics of other plastic and paper recycling schemes.

In order to address environmental issues, companies therefore need to address both the facts surrounding their impacts on the environment and the perceptions of these impacts. This requires companies to obtain a thorough understanding of their emissions and the wastes they dispose of, the effects of these emissions

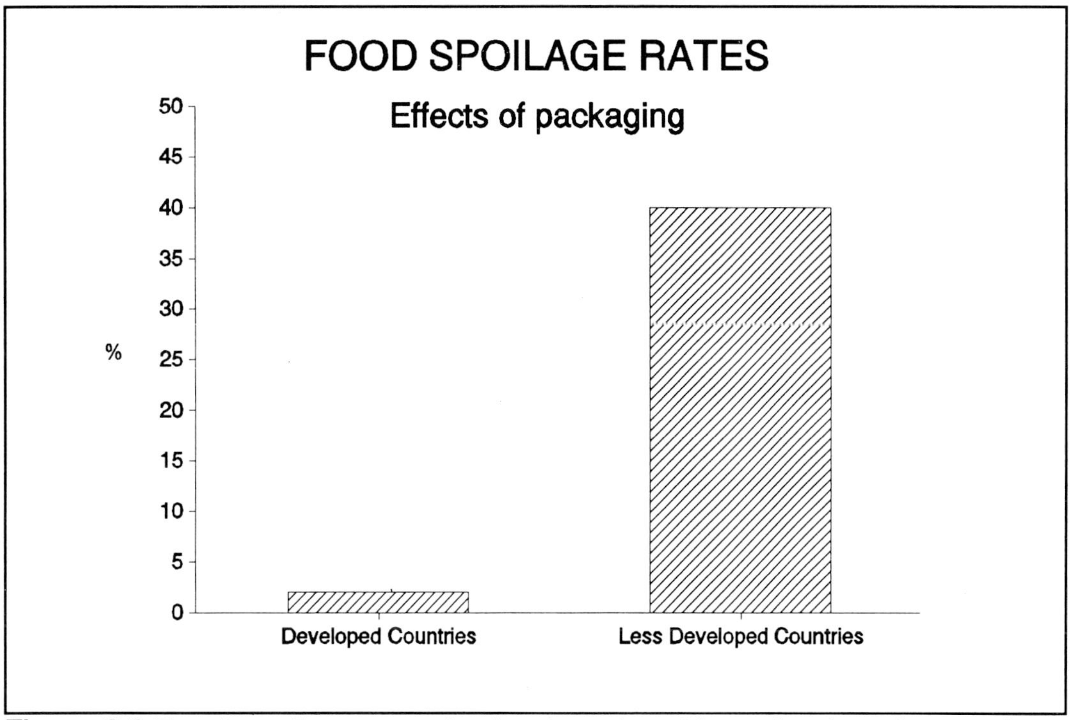


**Figure 2.3** Food spoilage rates in developed and less developed countries

on sectors of the environment, and the scientific basis for this understanding. It also requires a knowledge of how these effects are perceived and how these perceptions might change. The latter involves establishing a dialogue with interest groups such as the local community, employees, customers, environmental pressure groups and other organisations potentially affected by the company's operations.

## Chapter 3

## HOW TO TURN THE PRESSURES INTO SUCCESS

Research into the responses of a wide range of businesses to the environmental pressures put upon them has identified several key themes. Responses varied from a very defensive, negative attitude to environmental pressures (in which the degree of pressure is considered by the company to be out of all proportion to the size of the environmental problem) to a very positive, proactive approach (based on anticipating and managing the pressures). In the former case, the response was not considered to be a competitive issue but more a matter of survival of the whole industry. In the latter case, the response was more a competitive issue, with companies vying with their competitors for the best environmental credentials.

The results of this research are illustrated in Figure 3.1 below:

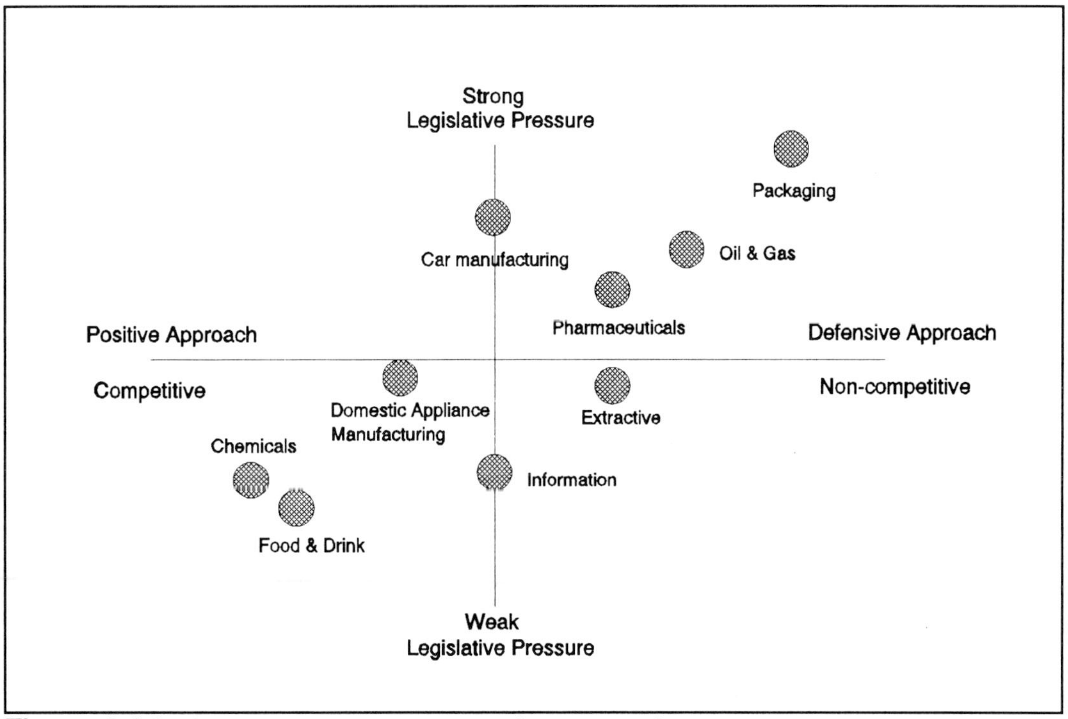


**Figure 3.1** Industry responses to environmental pressures

This shows the industry sectors sampled against two axes: one measuring the strength of the environmental legislative pressures they considered themselves to be under, and the second measuring their response to these pressures. Thus, while the chemical industry is subject to considerable environmental legislation, it has been the subject of legislation for some years and has adapted to it. On the other hand, the information industry has not been the subject of

significant environmental legislation. The legislative pressures can also take a number of forms. For example, for the car industry there is pressure on both the products produced and the processes which produce them.

The results indicate a correlation between the degree of legislative pressure an industry sector feels itself to be subject to and its response to these pressures. Essentially, once the general levels of environmental awareness and concern in society reach the level at which legislation is demanded, and is prepared by the legislators, then it is often too late for companies to have a significant influence on the shape of this legislation, and the only response remaining is a defensive one, with individual companies fighting against the legislation through trade bodies representing all the members' interests.

On the other hand, companies which are aware of concerns in society and address these at an earlier stage can avoid the need for legislation, or help to shape it in such a way that they can more easily accommodate its demands. They then have greater freedom to plan their own strategies, which may involve using environmental issues to gain advantage over their competitors.

The general picture is illustrated in Figure 3.2.

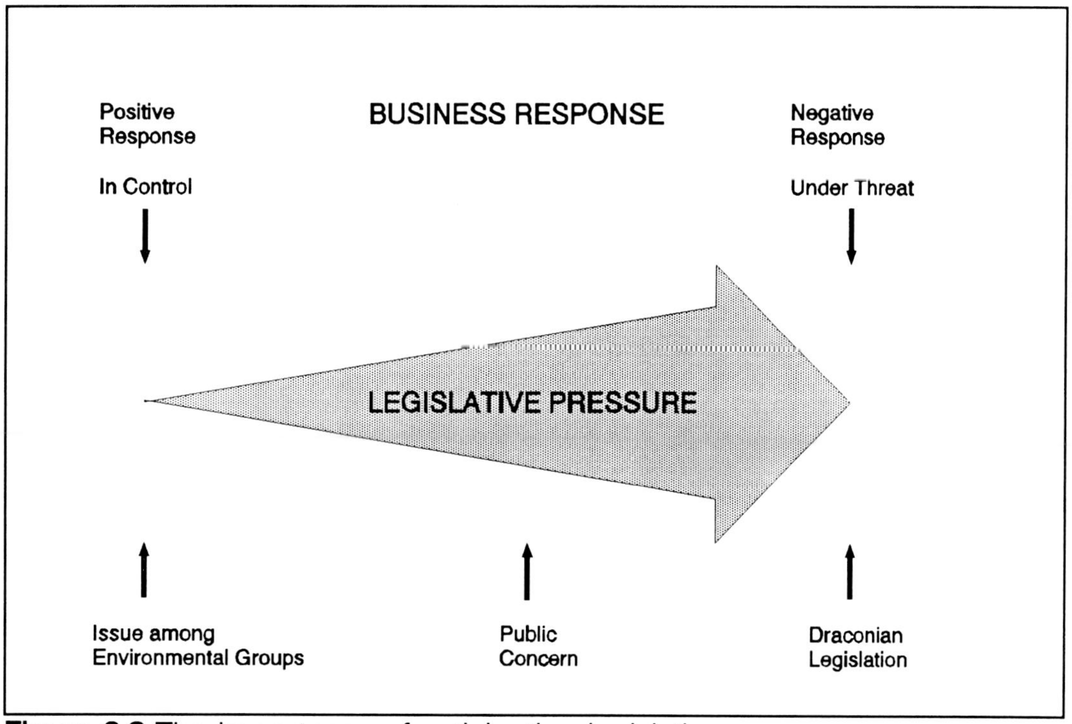


**Figure 3.2** The importance of anticipating legislative pressures

The analogy has been drawn with surfing: if you get in front of the wave it is easy to continue to ride it, but it is very difficult to catch the wave if you are behind it. The same is true of the environmental wave. If you anticipate the pressures while they are still small, it is possible to manage them. However, if you wait for legislation it will be too late and you risk falling off your surf board and drowning.

Most importantly, it is necessary to recognise that environmental pressures are driven as much, if not more so, by perceptions as by the facts of environmental harm. A familiar cry is that the public does not understand the issues. This may be true but in the environmental field as in many others there are rarely many 'right answers'. The importance attached to, for example, global warming relative to the loss of habitat of some rare species involves value judgements and the public's value judgements will be as valid as those of any eminent scientist. In these circumstances, companies which insist that they are right and the public are wrong are unlikely to succeed.

In summary, the businesses which succeed under growing environmental pressures will be those which:

- understand the issues:
    - amongst environmental pressure groups
    - of concern to the public
    - for the regulators
    - in different countries
- take account of perceptions of the issues as well as the facts
- act in advance of legislation

The following chapters document examples of companies which have followed some of these rules to achieve improvements in environmental performance at the same time as business success.

## Chapter 4

# TOTAL ENVIRONMENTAL MANAGEMENT

Environmental issues affect every aspect of business operations and each employee needs to play his or her part in achieving improvements. To address environmental issues most effectively, companies therefore need to integrate their approach to these issues throughout the business. Only a limited amount can be achieved by one or two individuals, and it is not sufficient to designate an environmental manager or create a small environmental unit to be responsible for the environment. Lasting and self-sustaining improvements can only be made if everyone in the organisation, from the operator of each part of each process right up to the senior managers, understands the impact of his or her actions on the environment and knows how and why to make improvements. This approach to resolving environmental pressures has been called total environmental quality management because of its similarities with the total quality management approach to quality in products and services.

The approach can only be implemented with the commitment of the senior management in the company, i.e. it needs to be top-down. However, once implemented, it allows initiatives to be driven from the bottom-up. Environmental issues have proved to be a strong motivator within companies, not only for the environment but also for quality and health and safety programmes, and quality programmes can often be more effective if linked to environmental as well as quality improvements.

Some examples are given below of companies which have successfully followed a form of the total environmental quality management approach to solving their environmental problems. In the process they have dramatically improved the efficiency of their processes, saving on the use of raw materials and energy and on the generation of waste, thus improving their environmental performance as a result. In all three cases, the companies now have structures and systems in place which encourage further improvements by harnessing the initiative of all the workforce.

## Example 1: Express Foods Creamery, Appleby, Cumbria

*Background*

Express Foods Creamery at Appleby in Cumbria was established in 1931 to pasteurise milk for transport by rail to London, but in 1971 production switched to cheddar cheese and whey products from the locally produced milk. Incoming milk is stored, pasteurised and then separated into curds and whey, the curds then being processed into cheddar cheese and the whey into whey concentrate,

whey powder and butter. The daily capacity of the factory is 400,000 litres of milk.

The liquid effluent from the factory is discharged to the foul sewer and treated in the local sewage treatment plant. In 1990, this effluent alone accounted for about 80% of the organic load and 60% of the volume of waste water treated at this sewage treatment plant. There had been pressure to increase production during the 1980s with little consideration of the effects this was having on the amount of effluent generated as a consequence. Eventually this led to breaches of discharge consent limits and a deterioration of relationships with North West Water Authority (NWWA) which operated the sewage treatment works. A new balance tank was installed, allowing the flow to be evened out over a 24-hour period to address this problem. However, although this helped to control the rate of discharge, it had no effect on the volumes or organic loadings produced. In addition to this effluent, stormwater drains for the site led directly to the local river, the River Eden, without treatment.

In 1987, an ammonia storage tank on the site for the refrigeration system sprang a leak. The tank was bunded, and consent was sought and obtained to discharge this ammonia into the effluent system. However, when the bund was emptied, it was emptied into the storm water drainage system by mistake. The resulting discharge of ammonia into the River Eden resulted in a large number of fish deaths and a record fine (£25,000) for the company. It also had to pay £112,000 for restocking the river. This incident marked a turning point for the factory in the management of its environmental responsibilities.

*The Appleby Experience*

The management team at the site recognised that a lasting improvement in the environmental performance of the factory depended on all members of the workforce playing their part. As a first step, an Effluent Awareness Committee was formed with representation from all departments and all levels of factory operations. This committee met weekly to consider the problems of effluent in some detail, such as its composition and origins, its environmental effects, and how it is managed elsewhere. The awareness of all representatives about the problems of effluent improved considerably as a result. Answers to many of the questions raised were soon identified, highlighting several critical areas requiring surveys and remedial action plans. Several problems were rectified (with little capital outlay) within weeks, and this success raised awareness and enthusiasm even more.

As a next step a graduate trainee was given the task of investigating the problems in more detail and recommending further improvements. This trainee studied the cleaning cycles (which make the greatest contribution to effluent), measuring the organic load and volume from each cycle and noting the timings

involved in each case. This information identified the sources of the strongest or largest volumes of effluent, and a priority action list was developed to reduce product and water losses, again at low cost. The data was also analysed using a computer program in order to estimate the contribution of predictable effluent and that associated with product spillages. Distribution of this information at meetings, on notice boards and even in the canteen helped to develop an entirely new attitude towards effluent and wastage control throughout the factory.

However, this enthusiasm needed to be coordinated, and a Production Services Department was then created, headed by an experienced manager, to take complete control of effluent issues. In addition, an Effluent Control Officer (ECO) was recruited from within the factory to be responsible for managing effluent discharges, and for developing and implementing a strategy for continual reduction in wastage and resulting effluent discharges. This was all achieved by June 1988.

In a matter of months this strategy paid dividends. Consent compliance improved and a better working relationship was developed with the NWWA. At the same time significant financial savings were made because of the reductions in wastage. In the first year these savings were:

| | £ |
|---|---|
| Detergent savings | 9,000 |
| Reduced NWWA trade effluent charges | 28,000 |
| Rebates for rainfall charged as trade effluent | 5,000 |
| Reduced water usage | 8,000 |
| Increased whey cream and powder yields | 30,000 |
| Total | 80,000 |

In subsequent years, specific wastage reduction projects were implemented to improve both the business and the environmental position further. Two examples serve as illustration:

**Milk reception.** This is the area where milk is delivered to the factory. Milk tankers transfer their load of milk to silos via hoses. After delivery the milk remaining in the hoses was lost when the hoses were uncoupled. This lost milk then simply entered the effluent drains. Considering that as many as 40 tankers unloaded each day, this amounted to a considerable wastage of raw material and added to effluent charges. The solution lay in an investment in stainless steel buckets. Operators were encouraged to carefully uncouple hoses, then drain the contents into these buckets and empty the buckets into a refrigerated

tank. At the end of each day, the tank contents were transferred to a silo for processing. The only cost involved was for the buckets and tank, and a payback was achieved for these in just 27 days.

**Reverse osmosis plant**. This plant pre-concentrates whey, prior to evaporation and drying, using semi-permeable membranes. The permeate which passes through the membranes becomes effluent. It is normally of relatively low strength, with little influence on trade effluent charges or compliance issues. However, these membranes eventually deteriorate, and milk solids then pass through, thus increasing the strength of the permeate. By introducing a careful monitoring procedure to test individual membranes and permeate strength, it is now possible to identify which membranes require replacement and to predict their individual life expectancy. This has proved to be a more efficient way of operating the plant and has resulted in savings of £30,000 per annum.

In total about £100,000 of capital expenditure has already generated £200,000 in savings and this progress is continuing. In 1990, the Effluent Awareness Committee became the Wastage Control Committee chaired by the ECO, who was also retitled the Wastage Control Officer to reflect new responsibilities which now also include energy, steam and paper. Other environmental issues including CFCs, stack emissions, noise and solid waste disposal are now also under review.

Express Foods discovered for themselves that ignoring environmental pressures can be a painful experience. However, mainly by raising awareness and changing attitudes, this experience has been transformed into benefits for both the environment and the business. The techniques developed at Appleby to monitor effluent and to control wastage are now adopted throughout Express Foods under the name 'the Appleby Experience'.

## Example 2: Thorn Lighting Limited, Spennymoor, County Durham

*Background*

Thorn Lighting Limited employs about 1100 people at its Spennymoor site and produces more than 2 million fluorescent light fittings per year from a range of more than 1800 different types and styles. The site also manufactures control gear for light fittings using an increasing number of electronic components. The site occupies 500,000 sq ft of building space on 32 acres of land and includes a new Research and Development Technology Centre.

Thorn Lighting has a commitment to the environment, health and safety which is expressed in the form of separate policies for the environment and health and safety, and through the development of a corporate environmental health and safety practices manual. The policy seeks to foster responsible care for the

environment in all aspects of the company's operations and to minimise progressively the environmental impact of its activities. It seeks not only to comply with environmental regulations, but also to be pro-active by initiating voluntary actions aimed at improving environmental performance. In particular, the policy includes the objective that Thorn Lighting will aim for the efficient use of energy, minimisation of waste and minimum use of non-renewable resources.

In 1990, Thorn Lighting was struggling with the effects of the recession and making a loss. Many savings and cost cutting exercises had already been made, the company had moved to Cellular Manufacture and 'World Class' manufacturing techniques, and was well on the way to being awarded BS 5750 (Part 1). The question was: where were further savings going to come from? Rather than allowing environmental issues to slip off the agenda because of these business pressures, the management instead started to look for solutions to the business problems in the company's environmental objectives.

*Resulting Achievements*

Some of the initiatives which resulted are described below:

**Energy conservation**. This is a major issue within Thorn Lighting. The programme began with the following measures:

- a consultant was employed to advise the company on energy conservation and energy management techniques

- a site energy team was formed

The consultant trained the energy team in auditing methods and information gathering techniques. The consultant's report recommended, firstly, a number of simple good housekeeping methods of conservation, such as turning off unwanted lighting, closing doors and windows, and repairing steam and air leaks. Secondly, it recommended low cost improvements such as lagging pipes, improving lighting switching arrangements and the use of more energy efficient lighting. Thirdly, there were recommendations for higher cost measures such as a change from steam heating to gas radiant heating, the introduction of smaller compressors and the introduction of an energy management system. Many of these measures have now been costed and budgeted for. Others have already been implemented and are resulting in savings.

**Water savings**. Water usage was highlighted as a major area for improvement in the energy survey. The survey identified the following areas in particular: excessive use of water in site washrooms, the inefficient use of mains water in rinsing operations and in cooling coils, and the lack of metering of trade effluent. Water is now recycled within the production process. Clean water is only used

where clean water is needed. It is then pH-adjusted and reused where water quality is not critical. These and other measures have already resulted in savings.

**Waste management**. Waste disposal methods were reviewed. Previously, dry waste, such as cardboard packing, computer paper, plastic sheeting, was collected together with general litter and stored in large open-topped skips before disposal by contractors. Similarly, scrap metalwork was collected together (regardless of its type) and sold as miscellaneous scrap. Following the review, the following measures were put in place:

- cardboard, computer paper and plastic sheeting is now collected in separate, marked containers, baled and sold for recycling
- suppliers are encouraged to deliver goods in returnable containers/pallets
- general waste is collected in small closed skips strategically placed and removed by the contractor without the need for any rehandling. This saves time and labour and prevents the escape of litter, thus saving on the need for litter patrols
- all scrap metalwork is now separated into clean, painted, etc, collected in marked containers and sold. The quantity and origin of the scrap is recorded in order to achieve better controls and set waste elimination targets

In addition, waste generation is now better controlled at source. Each manager has been made responsible for minimising waste generated in their areas and each has a waste budget to work to. Achieving this budget necessitates an evaluation of the potential for recycling, reuse and minimisation of all wastes in each area and taking active steps to reduce the volume of waste for final disposal. This project has highlighted the need for training of all staff in the importance of waste management. A specific training programme is being developed, and it is the company's intention to train all employees within one year.

**Environmental management manual**. Following an environmental audit, Thorn and its consultant drafted a Health, Safety and Environment manual which is applicable to the company as a whole. The emphasis, of the manual and the management systems underlying it, is on a total quality approach involving culture change throughout the workforce. Production is organised around cells, and each cell has its own production and quality targets and wastage budget. Returns are made on a shift by shift basis and there is regular publication and monitoring of the results. Continuous improvement is achieved by continually tightening the targets and budgets.

The effects of these measures on effluent discharge volumes and on the amounts of wastage for the site are shown in Figures 4.1 and 4.2.

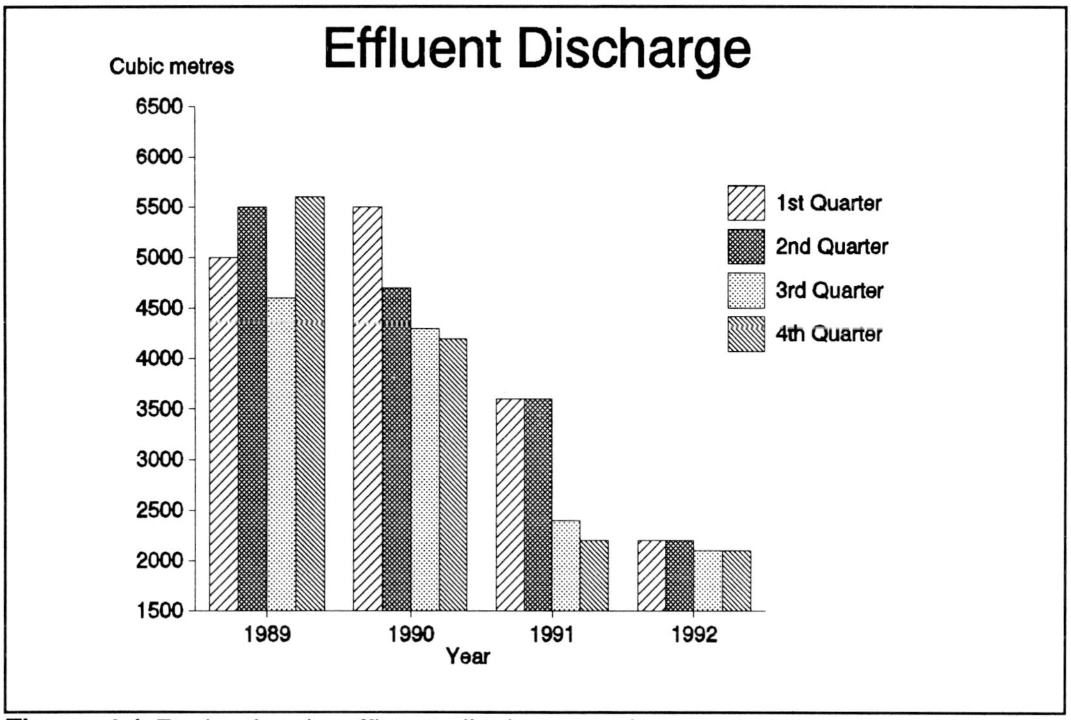


**Figure 4.1** Reduction in effluent discharge volumes

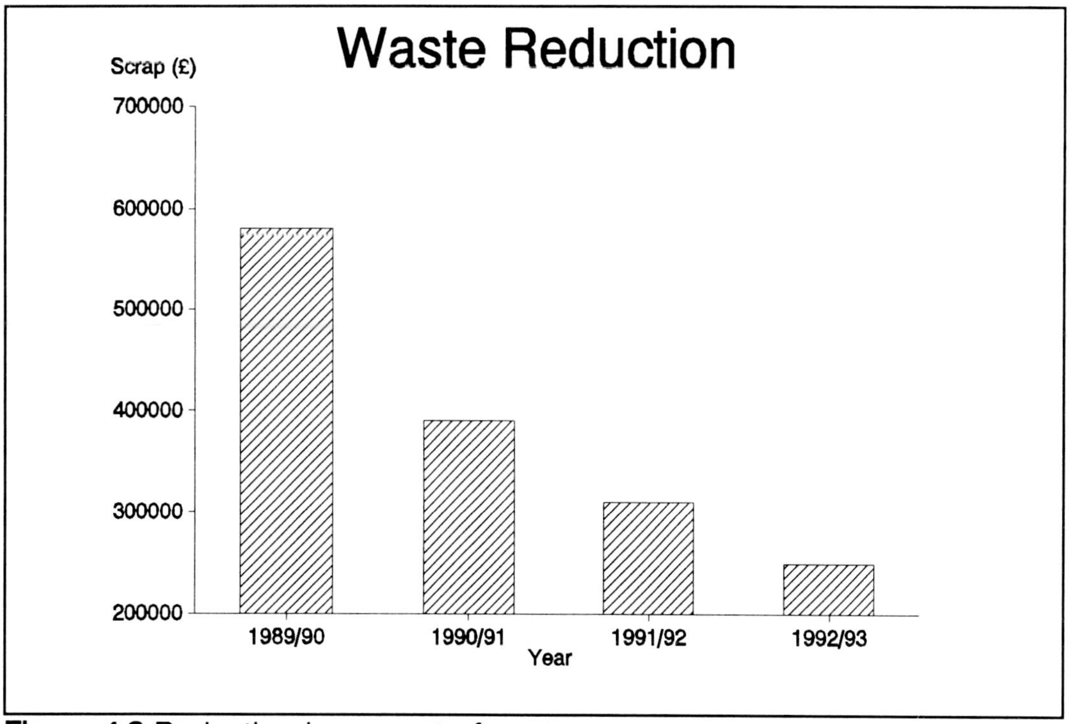


**Figure 4.2** Reduction in amount of wastage

The savings in 1991/92 and the projected savings in 1992/93 are shown in the following table.

| | Savings (£000s) | |
|---|---|---|
| | **1991/92** | **1992/93** |
| Waste clearance | 14 | 14 |
| Waste minimisation | 77 | 65 |
| Water management | 8.9 | 19 |
| Packaging changes | 37 | 74 |
| Energy management | 0 | 28 |
| Total | 136 | 201 |

Projected future savings from budgeted energy conservation projects are expected to amount to a further £218,000.

## Example 3: Harris Distribution, Slough

*Background*

Harris Distribution is a warehousing, transport and logistics Operating Division of TDG, Transport Development Group plc. In 1984, its Automated Warehouse Division was planning to build and operate a new warehouse in Slough for a major food product manufacturer. The warehouse would need to be able to store and manage the movement of 410,000 pallets, or 29.5 million cases, of product per annum on a 360 days-per-year, 24 hours-per-day operating basis. When the warehouse project was under consideration, environmental impact was seen as a critical factor in its commercial success. In addition, the company had a commitment to corporate quality and environmental excellence through its people. Although the project would represent the state-of-the-art in automated warehouse design, the company recognised the important contribution which the company's staff could make towards achieving the aim of best environmental practice.

*The Warehouse Project*

Environmental issues were considered at every stage of the warehouse project from design, through building and commissioning, to operating. The main environmental impacts of a large warehouse relate to the use of energy, vehicle

movements and their associated pollution and noise problems, and its visual impact. Some of the features of the warehouse design, which were developed specifically to address these issues, include:

**Energy.** The warehouse was designed to minimise the use of energy. Operations were fully automated to reduce space and lighting requirements. This also improved safety and dramatically reduced the potential for damaging product, pallets and plant (in the last year only 365 cases out of the 29.5 million handled arrived damaged at their destination). In addition, an energy conservation system in the warehouse air conditioning is currently providing a 1–2% saving on the electricity bill, and the introduction of an energy consumption monitoring system has led to an estimated £20,000 saving.

**Vehicle movements.** To prevent vehicle build-up and improve off-loading of vehicles, systems have been installed to signal the arrival of vehicles and off-load them automatically. This has resulted in a reduction in the dwell time of vehicles from an average of 1–3 hours for a non-automated warehouse to approximately 5–7 minutes. Routes have been chosen to keep vehicles away from residential areas and to minimise vehicle movements. Noise from the site has also been addressed by the construction of noise retaining boundaries.

**Visual impact.** This was addressed by minimising the warehouse footprint, including measures to reduce the use of space, and by carefully designing the location of equipment, such as siting sprinkler tanks under the warehouse floor.

### *The Importance of People*

All of these design features are only part of the story, however. The dynamic impetus for further year-on-year improvements has been provided by the warehouse staff.

Harris Distribution is committed to a people-oriented approach to both quality and environmental excellence. All site managers are given an environmental objective in their annual appraisal and when setting their targets for the next year. All new employees receive a full briefing on environmental issues when joining the company. Any employee can identify an area for environmental improvement through a report sheet. The Slough warehouse site, in particular, was pioneering the link between quality systems and environmental management, and environmental quality has been a key element of the operation and in the continuing improvement of the warehousing system.

To supplement the formal management systems which were developed for the site, the site manager also took a number of very subtle steps to raise environmental awareness amongst the site staff. These included placing notices on noticeboards about environmentally related programmes on the television

which might be of interest to staff.

The results have been impressive, with most environmental initiatives at the site now originating from the bottom-up, through the report sheet system. Following one suggestion, the site moved from the use of CFC propelled lubricants to an automatic lubrication system. This is estimated to have saved £1715 per year. Further energy-saving measures have been identified, and other initiatives include schemes for the recycling of computers, fork-lift truck batteries, paper, waste oils, dispatch folders and scrap metals. In many cases, the initiatives have also resulted in health and safety improvements.

Finally, as an example of the commitment and enthusiasm of the staff, each shift of four workers has organised a car sharing scheme for transport to and from work. This covers, in particular, route planning to minimise the distances travelled.

All the savings made at the site are passed on to the customer, making the company's services more competitive, and also ensuring continuing business for Harris. The site has won several awards for environmental achievements. In addition, during 1993, the Harris Distribution site at Slough became the first organisation to go through an external assessment to the new British Standard for Environmental Management Systems, BS7750, under the SGS Yarsley 'Green Dove Award Scheme'.

## Chapter 5

# WASTE MANAGEMENT

Waste is an inevitable product of every activity, but it is also an indication of less than perfect efficiency in converting input raw materials into useful output products. It is in the interests of every business to be as efficient as possible and therefore to minimise waste. Good waste management has as its aim the production of the most output with the generation of the least waste.

However, waste minimisation can take a number of forms. It can involve the redesign of a process to make it more efficient (i.e. a so-called 'cleaner technology'), it can involve recycling of materials either within the process or by using waste from one process as a raw material in another process, and it can involve developing new uses for materials which previously went to waste. However, care is needed to avoid pursuing recycling for its own sake without considering all of its implications. Recycling processes also generate wastes and in some circumstances these wastes can cause greater environmental problems than the original wastes being recycled. In addition, recycling often involves transport of materials and this can have greater environmental impacts than would arise from disposal of the wastes. Finally, collection of potentially recyclable material is of little use if there is no market for any products made from the collected material.

Therefore it is clear that waste management requires a holistic and carefully considered approach. Waste management hierarchies which set out the basic principles have been developed. In particular, the order of priority for options to deal with waste material is as follows:

- minimisation of the generation of waste at source
- reuse of the waste materials within the process
- reuse of the waste materials in another process
- recycling of the waste materials into other useful products
- incineration of the waste materials with recovery of useful energy
- treatment of the waste to make it less environmentally harmful
- disposal of the waste

Later chapters give examples of companies which have benefitted by applying particular steps in this hierarchy. However to begin with, an example is given of a company which has adopted a comprehensive approach to its waste management problem using elements of all of these steps.

## Example 4: Marks and Spencer plc

*Background*

In 1989, with the costs of disposing of the wastes generated in its stores and distribution centres rising above £1 million per year, Marks and Spencer decided to take action. At the time, Marks and Spencer was also facing increasing environmental pressure over the amount of packaging used to protect its goods, both in the stores and in distribution to the stores. It chose one of its distribution centres, that in Hayes, Middlesex, and the stores it served, and began a thorough investigation of the sources and types of waste being generated. The Hayes distribution centre was chosen because of its disproportionately high disposal costs: it contributed 8% of company sales but 13% of its refuse disposal costs.

The study carried out at Hayes and its associated stores identified several areas where potentially valuable materials were being thrown away as waste. These materials could be recovered and sold instead, but recovery of the material would need to be more efficient and much better segregation of the different types of material would be necessary. The company decided to carry out a pilot exercise at Hayes and its stores to see what kind of savings it could achieve.

*The Pilot Exercise*

The target set for Hayes and its stores was a saving of £50,000 in waste disposal costs in the first year. In addition, each store was given a smaller waste disposal budget than it had in the previous financial year.

A number of measures were investigated to reduce waste disposal costs:

**Improved waste segregation**. All waste materials from the stores and distribution centre were being treated in the same way: they were baled or compacted and disposed of. The review highlighted that many of these waste materials were potentially valuable if properly segregated. A better management system was introduced where segregation of materials was made easier.

Much of the waste generated in stores is plastic and paper. This is now segregated as it is generated. In the main receipt area and on each floor, there are separate containers for cardboard, polyethylene garment overbags, plastic trays and other mixed paper and plastic. In the office areas, there are separate containers for computer paper, till rolls and other paper. The segregated waste is collected in the store receipt area in empty delivery cages, and when a new delivery is made the waste is sent back to the distribution centre in the delivery lorry.

At the distribution centre there is also segregation of waste as it is generated. Cardboard waste from boxed goods is separated from mixed paper and plastic waste; polyethylene garment overbags and polypropylene security seals (estimated to amount to 650,000 at the Hayes distribution centre alone) are separately collected. A baler has been installed at the distribution centre to compact the polyethylene bags collected. The separated cardboard, paper, compacted polyethylene, and boxes of polypropylene seals and plastic hangers are collected from the distribution centre by recycling companies.

**Review of packaging composition.** Paper identification labels on polyethylene overbags and on shelf display trays reduced the value of the recovered material. Trials were conducted into the suitability of labels made from the same material as the overbags or trays. The aim was to improve the quality of the recovered material and to increase the range of uses to which it can be put, thereby increasing the value of the material to Marks and Spencer. However, because of the decline in the value of polyethylene, this concept did not progress beyond the trial stage, although it is now being reconsidered.

**Rationalisation of the use of materials.** Three types of shelf display trays were in use in the stores: those made of PVC, PET and OPS. Staff did not have the time or the knowledge to segregate them at source and a mixed plastic waste resulted. The company has now changed to only PVC trays so that segregation is now no longer necessary. However, recycling of the trays is currently not economically viable.

**Review of packaging strategies.** Across Marks and Spencer, distribution to stores is via distribution centres, each of which serves a number of stores. The number of stores served depends on the area of the country and the turnover of each store varies widely. Decisions about the optimum number of items to pack in a box for transport to a distribution centre then become very complex. Marks and Spencer has carried out modelling of this problem to help minimise the amount of packaging used.

**Review of collection frequency of compacted waste.** Most stores did not know whether the skips in which compacted waste was collected were full or empty when collections were made. Dispensing with unnecessary collection saves on waste transport, with associated environmental and cost benefits. It was estimated that reducing the number of collections in the London area by one per week would result in savings of £5000 per year.

**Store initiatives.** Stores have been encouraged to think creatively about ways of reducing waste. Cut flower buckets are now used as cleaning buckets, as waste bins and as storage containers for display tags. In one store, wall display units are sent to a local art college for use by students.

**Providing a market for recycled material.** Marks and Spencer has also used its

influence with the British Plastics Federation to encourage greater use of recycled plastics and is actively looking at ways to increase the number of items made from recycled materials in its stores.

*The results*

Net savings of £20,000 were made within a few months of the start of the pilot exercise and reductions in costs by 50% were expected over the whole financial year. This would translate into savings of £500,000 per year across the whole company. Instead of paying for the disposal of waste, the company was receiving payment for its recovered material. As an example, £100 costs per compacter to dispose of cardboard waste was turned into £25 earnings per compacter for recovered cardboard material for recycling.

Because of the success of the pilot exercise, similar measures were introduced across the whole company. However, recent developments in the market for recycled paper and plastic, as a result of German packaging legislation, have considerably reduced the resulting benefits. Instead of earning an income from sale of the recovered material, the company moved to a position of merely recovering its costs, and it is now continuing with the programme only for moral and social reasons, since the economic advantages have evaporated. Nevertheless, Marks and Spencer is in a better position than it would have been (i.e. without its waste management programme) to meet future changes in legislation and cost structures relating to waste disposal and recycling.

## Chapter 6

## WASTE RECOVERY AND REUSE

In the waste management hierarchy discussed in the previous chapter, reduction of waste at source should be the first option investigated, followed by recovery and reuse of products or materials. With increasing environmental awareness, there has been a focus on recycling, while reuse of products or materials has been comparatively neglected. Reuse is almost invariably less damaging to the environment than recycling because it involves less processing, with its consequential use of energy and generation of waste. In the 'throw-away' society, refurbishment and reuse of products are seen as too complicated and time-consuming, but reuse often offers an elegantly simple solution to a particular waste problem, as the following two examples illustrate.

### Example 5: Sainsbury's

*Background*

Carrier bags for customers to put their shopping in have been provided by supermarkets for many years in response to customer demand. Sainsbury's used to charge customers for these, but in 1984, because of customer pressure and the actions of its competitors, it introduced a smaller 'carry out' bag which was offered free to customers spending more than £20. In 1988, again in response to customer pressure, this £20 requirement was removed, and bags were offered free to all customers.

In the previous five years, the number of plastic carry out bags issued by Sainsbury's had increased by nearly 1000% to 12 million per week. During that time, retailers were coming under increasing environmental pressure from customers, pressure groups and legislation, particularly on the subject of packaging waste. Plastic carry out bags were perceived as an increasing source of waste and it was estimated that 2.5% of all plastic produced in the UK was used in the manufacture of carry out bags.

While Sainsbury's had already moved towards the use of post-consumer recycled plastic in its carry out bags, often using Sainsbury's own waste, it was clear that the increasing use of these bags, with the energy used in their manufacture and their contribution to waste, was not improving the environment. The bags were also perceived as a prime source of litter and thus added to the pressures on Sainsbury's and many other companies to address the issue of packaging waste. In addition, customers often saw the environmental problems of the bags as solved if the used bags were returned to the used plastic bag collection boxes available in stores.

*The 'Penny Back' Scheme*

In February 1991, Sainsbury's launched its 'Penny Back' scheme. This involves Sainsbury's offering customers a refund of 1p for every carrier bag which the customer brings back to the store and reuses for their shopping. The bag does not have to be a Sainsbury's bag to qualify for the refund. Customers are also offered the opportunity of donating the refunded money to charity.

Sainsbury's hoped to achieve a reduction in the number of new bags they would need to purchase and give away, thus providing benefits to both the environment and to the business. In addition, by encouraging reuse (as opposed to recycling) Sainsbury's aimed to raise awareness about the benefits of reusing carry out bags.

The objective of the scheme was to reduce the number of new plastic carry out bags issued by at least 50 million a year. This would save about 1000 tonnes of plastic and over 1 million gallons of oil, if transport and distribution impacts are included. As each carry out bag cost about 3p to produce, it would also save Sainsbury's about £1 million.

For the scheme to work effectively, it relies on staff to remember to offer money back and on customers to be aware of the offer and to bring bags back to the store. The launch of the scheme was therefore accompanied by publicity for customers (in the form of leaflets and posters) and badges for the check-out staff, plus a training programme for staff.

The success of the scheme was monitored from the check-out tills, by the amount of money collected for charity and by the reduction in the number of new bags issued. Experience clearly varied from one store to another, largely due to variations in the commitment of the store manager and the enthusiasm of the staff, and the scheme has needed periodic refreshment to ensure its continued success. However, experience with the scheme indicates that its objectives are being exceeded, with annual savings reaching 59 million carry out bags.

### Example 6: Inkwell (UK) Limited, Chew Stoke, Bristol

*Background*

Ink-impregnated fabric ribbons have been used to produce printed text since the earliest typewriters were invented. Even today with inkjet and laser printers, the market for fabric printer ribbons is still considerable. Most cash registers, parking ticket machines and cash dispensers use fabric ribbons and they are still in widespread use in computer printers on workhorse impact printing machines.

Fabric printer ribbons are currently manufactured by passing wide rolls of nylon through vats of thick ink. Excess ink is squeezed out by large rollers and the ribbon is then cut to size. The printers work by transferring ink from the ribbon on to the page. Once the ink has been used up, the ribbon is replaced and the old ribbon is traditionally thrown away.

One day, Julie Wright was using her word processor and printer when the printer ribbon 'ran out'. She duly replaced it and threw the old ribbon away. Her father, who happened to be with her, felt this was a waste. He inspected the used ribbon and decided that it should be possible to re-ink the fabric. Using a fishing reel and wooden off-cuts, a crude re-inking device was constructed which worked, and Inkwell was born.

*Inkwell*

The re-inking machine developed by Inkwell from the prototype relied on thinning the ink sufficiently for it to be sprayed on to the ribbon. This spraying process could then be controlled by computer to ensure that the amount of ink was optimal. Patents were taken out on the design of the re-inking machine, which was developed through a number of versions. The Mark IV version was the first real production machine and came into operation in early 1991. It could cope with over 80% of the fabric ribbon market and could handle about 20 operations per hour.

The machine was the only industrial ribbon re-inker in the world and the only machine able to re-ink cassetted, reel-to-reel and stuffed ribbons, and to do so in a variety of colours. The quality of the re-inked ribbons was as good as, and in some cases better than, new ribbons.

The company offered a re-inking service to customers. Instead of throwing their used ribbons away, customers were provided with a specially designed box into which they placed the ribbons. Once the box was full, it was sealed and a freepost label used to post it to Inkwell. The ribbons were re-inked within two working days and then posted back to the client. The cost of the re-inked ribbons was 50% of the cost of new ribbons and their quality was just as good. The ribbons could be re-inked up to 10 times before the quality failed to meet quality checks.

Within two years the company had over 200 customers for its re-inking service including small, medium and large companies and was anticipating a turnover of £5 million. The reuse of the ribbons was also saving on the number of ribbons entering the solid waste stream, estimated at 14 million plastic cassettes annually in the UK alone.

However, Inkwell has since become a victim of its success. Increasing demand for its services outstripped its ability to provide a viable re-inking service with its current technology. Being a small company with limited funds, it eventually ran out of time to develop a better machine. Inkwell unfortunately ceased operating in early 1993.

## Chapter 7

## BYPRODUCT UTILISATION

The next question to be asked after 'can this waste product be reused?' is 'can this waste product be converted into something that can be used or sold?'. By considering what useful products can be made from the waste material, one is finding a true solution to the waste disposal problem, because this route explicitly addresses the issue of the market for the recycled material. The material is either used in-house or it is sold as a valuable product in its own right. This approach has been called 'byproduct utilisation' because it treats waste material as a byproduct of the process which can be turned into useful product. At the same time, consideration is given in the choice and design of the recycling process to the products which will be produced and the use to which they will be put. The following examples illustrate how genuinely useful products can be produced profitably from material which has previously been classed and disposed of as waste.

### Example 7: Haden MacLellan Holdings plc, Egham, Surrey

*Background*

The production of paint sludge is an inevitable byproduct of high volume paint spraying operations, such as those carried out in the car industry. The waste paint sludge is usually disposed of by landfill or incineration, despite containing solvents and heavy metals. In a typical paint shop, only about 50% of the paint applied actually hits the target and wastage is therefore high. About 10 kg of paint sludge is produced on average per vehicle. The total amount of paint sludge produced each year by the car industry alone in Western Europe is estimated at 110,000 tonnes.

Haden MacLellan is one of the foremost suppliers of high volume paint shops. With the growing awareness of environmental issues, the company decided in 1985 to find a solution to the problem of paint sludge disposal. The aim was to develop a more environmentally acceptable system for dealing with the sludge which could be sold to the car plants and other large scale users.

Many previous attempts had been made to dry paint sludge but all had failed because of the sticky nature of the material. Haden MacLellan's research was therefore aimed at finding a drying method which would prevent heat transfer surfaces from becoming fouled and which would allow drying to take place in an oxygen-free environment to prevent fires. The objective was to turn wet, sticky, potentially hazardous paint sludge into a dry inert powder which could be recycled. Various forms of drying were attempted during the research before the

method finally adopted was conceived in 1986.

*The 'DryPure' Process*

The process developed by Haden MacLellan, called DryPure, is designed to evaporate the water vapour and solvents in the paint sludge and then to cure the residual paint resin systems. The curing process encapsulates any harmful materials within these resins. The exhaust gases which evaporate during drying are oxidised to ensure a clean, odourless discharge, but much of the resin system remains, and carbon dioxide emissions are therefore minimised. The fume incinerator, where the exhaust gases are burnt, provides most of the heat required for the drying process.

A pilot plant was built which was capable of handling 150 kg/hr of wet sludge, in order to prove the effectiveness of the process. This is approximately equivalent to a 15 vehicle-per-hour automotive paint shop.

Following completion of satisfactory pilot plant trials, the first commercial installation was completed at the Chrysler, Warren Truck plant in Detroit, USA during the summer of 1988. The fact that the first installation was in the USA was a reflection of the greater environmental pressures on companies in the USA at the time. The plant has operated successfully since then.

The dry powder resulting from the process can be used as an inert filler in various coatings, sealants, mastics and sound deadening materials. In particular, a sprayed underbody sealant was formulated using the powder produced at Warren Truck and it is undergoing long-term trials with a view to its use at the same plant.

The product also has a high calorific value and has been used as a fuel in cement kilns. However, the suitability of the product for this use depends on the origin of the sludge, and use as a fuel is not seen as ideal. Other uses which have been investigated include roofing materials and a return to low-grade paints.

Soon after the proven success of the Warren Truck plant, four more drying lines were commissioned at General Motors (Texas), EPI (Toledo, Ohio) and Jaguar Cars Ltd (Birmingham, UK). The plant at Jaguar handles all sludge produced by Jaguar and allows other interested companies to try the process on their paint sludges.

Europe is seen as the next major market for this process, with a great deal of interest from EC countries and Scandinavia. There has also been considerable interest from major companies in Japan in licensing the technology. Expected stricter legislation on disposal of hazardous materials in landfills can only help to

increase demand for the process.

**Example 8: Matsushita Electric (UK) Ltd**

*Background*

Matsushita Electric (UK) Ltd, perhaps better known as Panasonic, manufactures televisions and microwave ovens. In 1991/92, over 1.3 million units were produced at its plants in Cardiff for distribution throughout the UK and Europe. The process of manufacturing these products is relatively clean and few hazardous wastes are produced.

However, with growing public awareness of the environment and the 1990 Environmental Protection Act, Matsushita recognised a need to look more closely at the waste it was producing and the ways it was disposed of. Of particular concern was expanded polystyrene, which is used to protect cathode ray tubes supplied to the Cardiff plant during transport. Upon delivery to Cardiff, this material became waste. The scale of the increasing problem is illustrated in Figure 7.1.

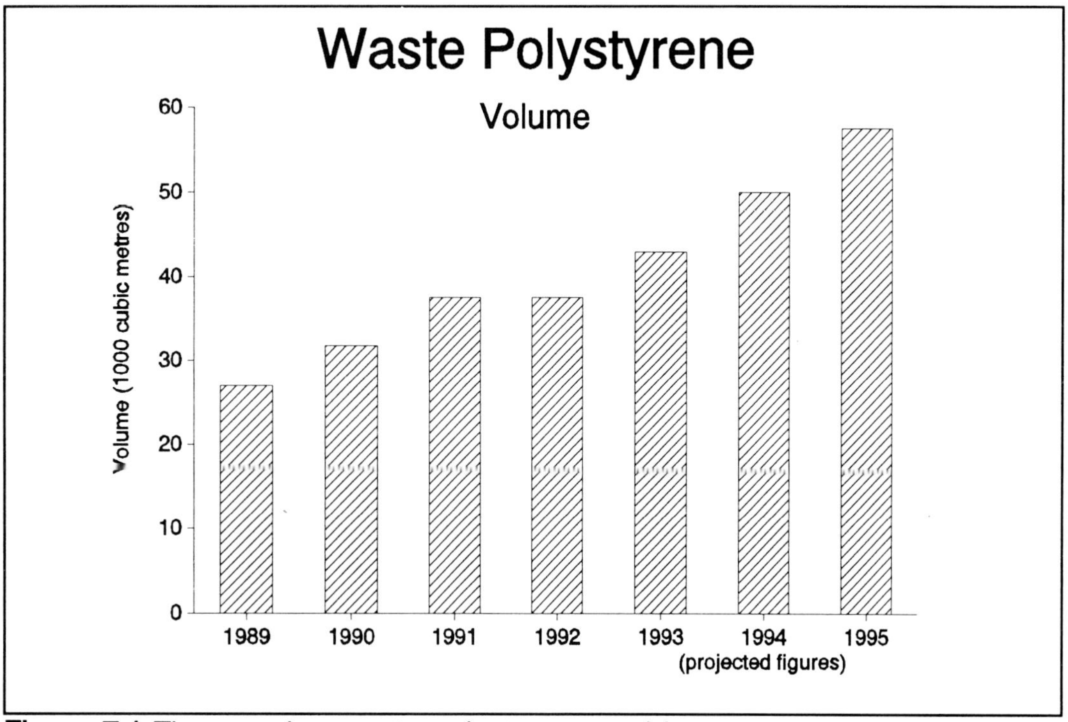


**Figure 7.1** The growing waste polystyrene problem

Until the early 1990s, some of this material had been collected by contractors for reuse as cavity wall insulation in buildings. The remainder was disposed of to landfill. However, with the recession in the building industry, demand for the material for use in cavity wall insulation dropped. Contractors started to ask for payment to take the material away and more and more material was having to be sent to landfill. The material caused particular problems (as far as landfill was concerned) because of its light weight. No tipping of the waste was allowed at all under certain weather conditions, and disposal was becoming costly. When disposal was not possible, the material had to be stored on site, and, when it was windy, this also resulted in environmental problems.

It was clear that a better solution to the problem of this polystyrene waste was needed. Matsushita investigated a number of options. For example, a hot melt system was considered, where the expanded polystyrene was melted into 1 kg solid blocks. However, this process proved to be too slow to cope with the volumes of polystyrene being generated at its site, and the capital expenditure needed to build a plant with a large enough capacity would have been too high.

*The Solution*

The solution eventually adopted involved the use of an innovative compaction system which reduces the volume of the material by a factor of 20. In its compacted form the material is easier to handle, and can be reused for the following purposes:

- production of more packing chips
- production of custom-shaped expanded polystyrene packing pieces by gas filling
- production of crystal polystyrene for use to injection mould new products

The compaction machine required was developed jointly by Matsushita and an outside supplier. The entire recycling process is shown in Figure 7.2.

The use of this system resulted in a cost saving of £60,000 in the first year, expected to rise to £65,000–70,000 per year once production at the Cardiff plant returns to capacity.

Additional benefits of the process include the avoidance of a large amount of the lorry transport (which had been required to collect the uncompacted material for either reuse or disposal). Transport movements have been reduced by 80%.

Not surprisingly, the new process is generating a great deal of interest from companies with similar problems in the UK and overseas.

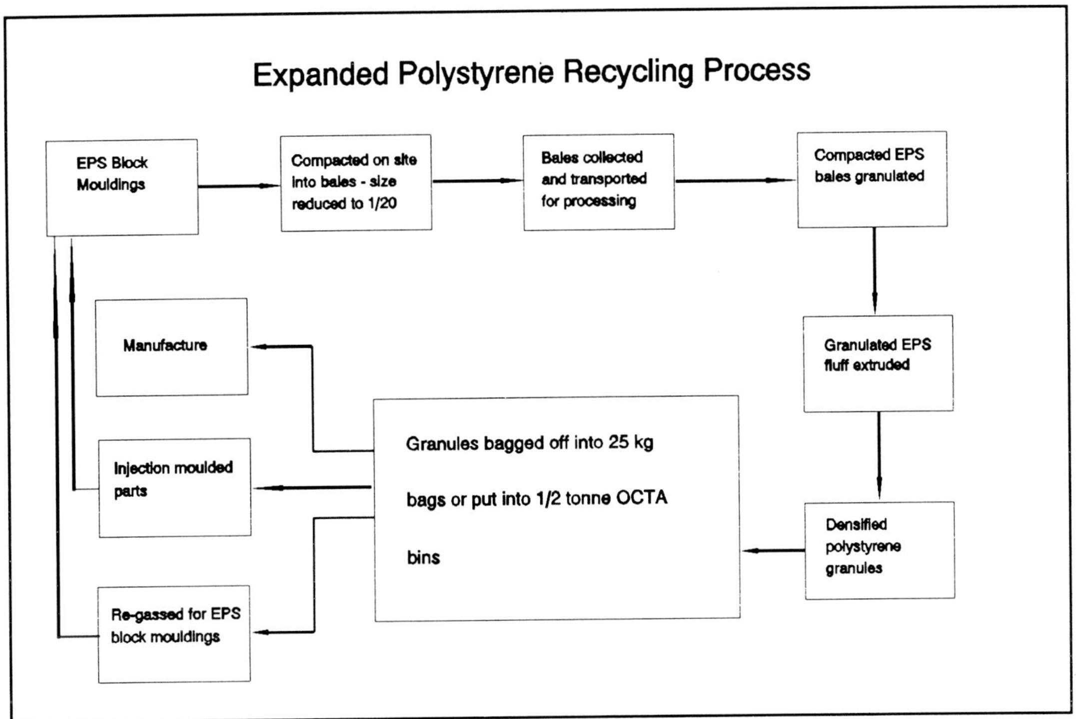


**Figure 7.2** The new polystyrene recycling process

## Example 9: AVX Ltd, Coleraine, Northern Ireland

*Background*

AVX make ceramic capacitors for the electronics industry. The company is the largest private employer in the region with about 1000 staff and it produces ten million multi-layer ceramic devices per day. It has an American parent which is in turn owned by the Kyocera Corporation of Japan.

The manufacturing process for the ceramic devices involves two major steps, namely, the burning-out of organic materials and subsequent high temperature firing, in order to achieve controlled component shrinkage and complete densification. The devices are fired in rectangular crucibles, called saggars, with cover plates, both of which are made out of alumina-based refractory material. These are occasionally damaged or broken and need to be replaced. However, new crucibles and cover plates need to be fired (filled with firing sand) several times before use, in order to be 'seasoned' with the specific type of ceramic material, and to minimise the interaction between the new 'furniture' and the unfired ceramic components. The broken or damaged crucibles are disposed of to landfill. The annual cost of new kiln furniture amounts to £48,000.

Fired capacitors then have their sharp corners or edges removed by a process of 'harperisation' using an alumina grinding powder. The waste slurry produced by this process, which is made up of alumina powder and excess material mechanically removed from the components, is washed down into a settling tank. After settling, this used to be sent for special disposal on the British mainland, because of its content of heavy metals. The settling tanks are emptied four or five times a year, producing 40 tonnes of waste each time. The cost of the alumina powder, which is used once, amounts to £18,000 per year, and the cost of disposing of the waste sludge is £12,000 per year.

With the environmental pressures on waste disposal growing, and in keeping with its strong environmental policy which was being enthusiastically implemented, the company investigated alternative solutions to this waste disposal problem.

*New Kiln Furniture*

Because the waste sludge from the grinding process is mainly alumina, which is also the main constituent of the kiln furniture, the possibility of utilising the waste alumina powder in the manufacture of kiln furniture was investigated. Because the waste contains components from the ceramic formulations used in the factory, its use in the crucibles and cover plates should minimise the risk of contamination and possible reaction with the ceramic devices and reduce the amount of seasoning that the new furniture will need. Because this furniture has a similar composition to the product being processed, it is known as 'semi-autogenous'.

Initial evaluation of this concept proved the feasibility of manufacturing kiln furniture (particularly the cover plates) from the recovered alumina grinding waste. This was followed by six months of on-line tests using cover plates made from the recycled alumina. These tests indicated the thermal cycling resistance of these cover plates was similar to that of commercially sourced cover plates. A contract was then negotiated with a local ceramics company to supply commercial quantities of kiln furniture made from the recovered alumina waste. The use of these was expected to result in savings of between £21,000 and £33,000 in the cost of new kiln furniture and in reduced disposal charges.

## Chapter 8

# CLEANER TECHNOLOGIES

So-called 'cleaner technologies' are based on the principle that prevention is better than cure. They are process technologies which are inherently more efficient in their use of energy and raw materials and less polluting in terms of the waste and emissions from the production processes involved. As a way of reducing the environmental impact of a process, they are clearly distinct from the more commonly available end-of-pipe technologies which concentrate on the treatment of the wastes produced, rather than on minimising the production of waste at source. Between these two distinct approaches there is also a grey area which involves recycling of materials, either within the process or in some other process. These technologies are sometimes also included within the definition of cleaner technologies. The concepts are illustrated in Figure 8.1.

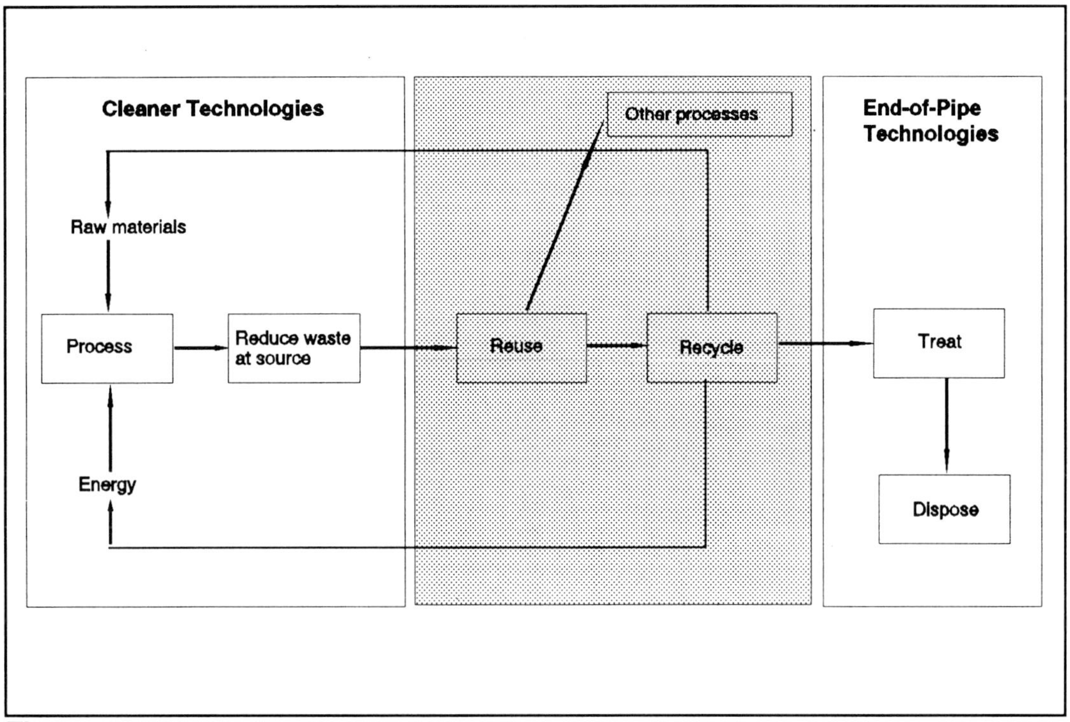


**Figure 8.1** Cleaner technology definitions

In general, cleaner technologies involve major changes to the process of interest. This process change is one of the main reasons why cleaner technologies are not as widely investigated or implemented as might be expected from a consideration of their economics. Because they involve more efficient use of energy and raw materials, they generally have commercial as well as environmental advantages. However, businesses are often reluctant to consider

environmental improvements in advance of a legislative requirement to do so. Because changes in legislation rarely coincide with a process upgrade, the only solution then available to a company faced with a legislative requirement to improve its environmental performance is a 'bolt-on' end-of pipe solution.

Companies which take a longer-term view and which consider the environmental implications and cleaner solutions when planning a process change or when introducing a new process almost invariably gain in business terms. They can be sure of meeting future changes in environmental legislation without needing to invest in end-of-pipe technology, and the cleaner technology is usually cheaper to operate because it is more efficient. There are often product quality benefits as well.

Processes can be made intrinsically cleaner in a number of ways. For example:

- by avoiding the use of environmentally damaging raw materials
- by recycling more process chemicals/raw materials within the process
- by controlling the process better, e.g. by using monitoring of process parameters and computer control to maintain optimum conditions
- by making better use of byproducts from the process, e.g. using waste gases to provide heat energy

Because they involve process changes, cleaner technologies require more up-front investment and greater risk than more conventional bolt-on solutions. However, the long-term benefits can quickly enable this investment to be recovered.

The following examples illustrate how the cleaner technology approach has been applied in a wide variety of industrial processes, with both environmental and business benefits.

### Example 10: Lucas Nitrotec Services Ltd, Birmingham

*Background*

Lucas Nitrotec Services Ltd, a wholly owned subsidiary of Lucas Industries plc, the manufacturer of components for the automotive industry, was established in 1988 specifically to market and develop a new process (the Nitrotec process) for surface treating low alloy and mild steels.

Traditionally, a combination of treatments has been used to make low-alloy and mild steels suitable for use in engineering applications, particularly in the automotive industry. Heat treatment is used to increase strength, hard chromium plating and electroless nickel plating are used to produce wear resistance, and electroplating with zinc, cadmium or nickel is used to give corrosion resistance.

All of these processes involve potential problems for the health and safety of operators, and for the environment, mainly in the form of liquid effluent and solid waste containing toxic elements. A further disadvantage of traditional heat treatment processes is that the thermal stress resulting from the very high temperatures causes distortion of large thin-sectioned components and prevents the production of lighter high-strength components. This was becoming increasingly important for the car industry with increasing pressures to reduce vehicle weight, in the interests of fuel efficiency, without sacrificing strength.

*Process Development*

Research work in the early 1980s encouraged a team at Lucas to believe that an all gaseous nitrocarburising process could be modified to impart strength and corrosion resistance simultaneously, and the team embarked on a development programme with the following goals:

- elimination of the substances which had the potential for polluting the local environment
- lowering of the treatment temperature to enable components to be reduced in weight in proportion to the enhanced strength

The nitrocarburising process showed promise because the diffusion of nitrogen into the steel which occurs and which gives the required strength could be produced at temperatures as low as 550°C. However, nitrocarburising was originally developed as a salt bath process and involved the use of cyanide, nitrate and possibly hydroxide compounds.

Gaseous nitrocarburising, carried out in a furnace, avoids these problems. It is based on the partial replacement of the normal carburising gases by ammonia, resulting in a 40% reduction in the carbon monoxide content of the furnace gases and lower carbon dioxide emissions in the vented combusted gases. However, with gaseous nitrocarburising, when cooling is carried out in the traditional manner by quenching in neat mineral oil, the surface has the required strength but is deficient in corrosion resistance. The quenching process involves the use of detergent washing or solvent degreasing (with their associated environmental problems), and the deficiency in corrosion resistance needs to be overcome with either electroplating or organic coating.

The breakthrough came with the discovery that controlled oxidation of the nitrided surface, followed by quenching in a water based emulsion instead of neat oil, produced an oxygen enriched layer with low frictional properties and outstanding corrosion resistance. This is the basis of the Nitrotec process, so-called because it combines the terms *NITR*ocarburising, *O*xidizing, pro*TEC*tion.

*Nitrotec Technology*

The process currently utilised by Lucas Nitrotec is based on the use of vacuum-purged electrically heated furnaces, which eliminate the use of carbon monoxide as a process gas and carbon dioxide as an emission gas, and allow much greater process control. After loading, the chamber is evacuated and backfilled with nitrogen so that all the components achieve process temperature in an oxygen-free atmosphere before nitrocarburising commences. Controlled amounts of ammonia and oxygen-bearing gases are then introduced to produce the surface and diffusion layers required.

Low-alloy and mild steel components treated with the Nitrotec process have the following enhanced properties:

- an increase in the yield and fatigue strength by up to four times, thus allowing thinner sections with the same strength and, hence, lighter components
- wear resistance superior to that obtained by hard chromium plating
- corrosion resistance better than that of zinc plating
- a black finish of pleasing appearance

*Environmental and Business Benefits*

Alternative processes include salt bath processes which involve the use of molten cyanides, high-temperature carburising processes involving the use of more carbon monoxide and mineral oils with their attendant fume and fire risks, electroplating processes which involve the use of corrosive chromic and sulphuric acids and metal cyanides, and electroless nickel plating which gives rise to effluents containing nickel and phosphorous compounds. All of these processes involve much higher risks to the health and safety of their operators and to the environment in the form of the liquid effluent and solid waste produced.

The Nitrotec process operates at a lower temperature and requires no effluent treatment and is therefore much cheaper than these alternatives. The process can also operate economically in a batch mode so that the service can be better tailored to demand.

As planned, the Nitrotec process has enabled high-strength components to be made with lower weight. The most notable example is the lightweight bumper armature developed for the Rover 800 car. The process enabled the vehicle to meet the stringent EC impact criteria while at the same time achieving a weight saving of 12 kg per vehicle. The process is also used on components in vehicles manufactured by Renault, Ford, Toyota and BMW.

The treatment process is offered as a service by Lucas Nitrotec. The company has only a small staff yet it has not neglected the future and continues to be involved in research and development of its process. It won the Queen's Award for Technological Achievement in 1992.

The company's income from sales of its services, as a percentage of capital investment, is shown in Figure 8.2.

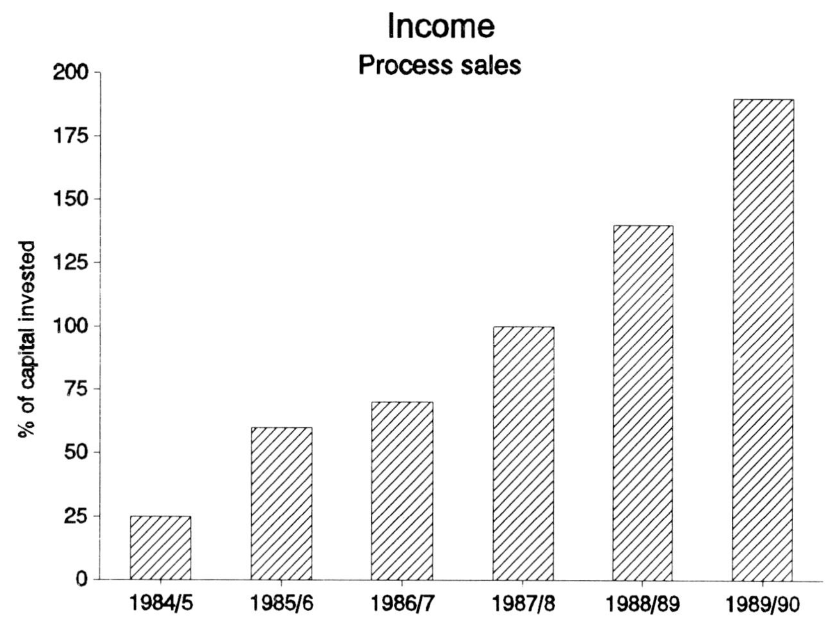


**Figure 8.2** Income from sales of Lucas Nitrotec services

Lucas Nitrotec has licensed its technology to companies in the UK, the USA, Japan, Australia, Italy, Denmark and Germany, selling 13 licences in five years, and the company is gaining a significant return in the form of royalty income. It is now entering into joint ventures, the first being in France and the second in the USA.

Although the origins of the process were in surface treatment for automobile components, the process is now also being used on components in equipment for the home and office. Examples include the magazine of a hand stapler and the cutting blade of a lawn-edge trimming device. An advanced treatment process, called Nitrotec S, in which the surface is polished, produces a finish which compares favourably with hard chromium plating and this has been used in piston rods. Other applications include the torque plates for the viscous differential, which can now be made much more cheaply.

The Nitrotec process improves resistance simultaneously to both wear and corrosion, the two problems which lead to more loss in engineering than any other failure mode. However, even Nitrotec treated components eventually fail, but when they do they are readily recyclable.

**Example 11: Zeneca Pharmaceuticals Ltd (formerly ICI), Macclesfield, Cheshire**

*Background*

In late 1986, Zeneca Pharmaceuticals acquired worldwide rights to develop and market its own brand of a heart drug discovered by an American pharmaceutical company. The drug is used to treat hypertension and congestive heart failure. Zeneca's brand is known as 'Zestril' and was launched in 1988.

The Macclesfield works of Zeneca employs about 1500 people and produces crude pharmaceuticals. Formulation into specific products is carried out elsewhere. Zestril was first manufactured there by Zeneca in a pilot plant in 1987. The process used was that developed by the American company, and was the process on which all product approvals had been based.

The manufacture of Zestril involves three stages prior to tablet formulation. The stages are:

- hydrogenation to produce an ester
- work up of an aqueous solution of the ester to produce crude bulk drug
- purification involving treatment with activated carbon

The work-up stage involves saponification of an aqueous solution of ester with caustic liquor and removal of low boiling point impurities by vacuum distillation. Hydrochloric acid is then added and the impurities removed by extraction with ethyl acetate. Salts are then removed from the aqueous solution. This is particularly difficult because the drug being manufactured is very soluble in water. The process involves passing the aqueous solution through a resin bead column which absorbs the drug. The salts are then washed through with water and the drug recovered from the resin beads with Industrial Methylated Spirit (IMS). The IMS solution is then reduced in volume by vacuum distillation and held until recrystallisation occurs. The product is finally filtered, washed and dried.

The pilot plant was successful in manufacturing the drug product. However, it was clear from the pilot plant that full-scale production would swamp existing effluent disposal routes and more than triple current waste disposal volumes and costs for the site. With increasing environmental pressures to reduce effluent discharges and waste, this was clearly unacceptable, and a programme was initiated to reduce waste from the process.

Improvements in the process are made more difficult in the case of drug manufacture because of the stringent controls placed on drug manufacturing processes and the requirements for complex and lengthy licensing procedures for new drugs. Every change to the manufacturing process requires the agreement of the licensing authorities.

*The Improved Process*

In the original process, process chemicals and water were generally used once only and then disposed of. In order to address the pollution problems of full-scale operation, Zeneca investigated ways of reducing this waste. It did this with a detailed and structured examination of the origins of the effluent and alternative processes. In particular, by reusing some of the process chemicals at other stages in the process, considerable improvements were possible. Considerable effort was devoted, in particular, to improving the operation of the resin column. This included increasing the concentration of IMS, improved process monitoring and recycling of wash water. In addition, more accurate control of distillation allowed extraction volumes to be reduced.

Zeneca also introduced the concept of the Effluent Load Factor (ELF), which was the volume of effluent produced in litres per kilogram of product. This was monitored and displayed on a regular basis and has provided a strong motivation for improvements by all involved in the process.

The result was a reduction in ELF by a factor of approximately three (from 694 to 247) by May 1991. Further improvements were being considered to reduce the ELF further to 85. These involved capital expenditure of around £150,000. Beyond these measures, concentration of the salt residues could bring the ELF down to about 8, and the use of reverse osmosis, rather than a desalination column, could reduce the energy used in the process and reduce volatile organic compound emissions. These options were under research.

More details of the resulting waste reductions and cost savings are given in the table on the next page. The total savings in effluent disposal costs amount to £400,000 per annum. In addition, solvent usage has been reduced to one third of its 1988 level, resulting in additional savings of £300,000 per annum.

The environmental impact of the process is now low enough that it meets environmental standards anywhere in the world. Further work will improve the process to the point where it is based on virtual total recycling of process chemicals and where it will have negligible environmental impact.

| Stream | Waste volume per tonne of product ($m^3$) | | Cost per tonne of product (£k) | |
|---|---|---|---|---|
| | Jan 1988 | May 1991 | Jan 1988 | May 1991 |
| Contract incineration | 145 | 4 | 15 | 1 |
| Contract treatment | 140 | - | 7 | - |
| Treatment at local sewage works | 200 | 260[a] | 3 | 1 |
| Total | 485 | 264 | 25 | 2 |

[a] Although the waste volume sent to the local treatment works increased, its strength is only 25% of the 1988 level.

## Example 12: Eastern Counties Leather plc, Sawston, Cambridge

*Background*

Eastern Counties Leather plc is currently embroiled in a landmark court case over the contamination of drinking water supplies as a result of its tanning operations in the 1960s, when, like most other industrial companies at the time, it allowed the chemicals it was using to spill and leak into the ground. In more recent years, it has taken a lead in cleaning up its site and its processes with commercial and environmental success.

Eastern Counties Leather is a small family-owned company founded in 1879. It operates from a site on the outskirts of the village of Sawston about 10 miles from Cambridge and employs about 75 people. Its raw material is sheep skins, byproducts of the meat industry, mainly from the UK and New Zealand. The skins are split, with the outer layer (or grain) being pickled for export to be made into leather goods, and the inner layer (or flesher) being tanned, degreased and made into chamois leather, mainly for car care. The company has a wide customer base in the UK and well-established distribution contacts overseas, where 80% of its products are exported.

A number of environmentally driven initiatives have been carried out to improve operations at the site. These include a more efficient use of space and the decontamination of areas of the old factory and surrounding land, recycling of pickling liquid and the construction of a new effluent treatment plant. However, the company's most interesting innovation concerns the development of a new process for degreasing skins after tanning.

Eastern Counties Leather had been degreasing its tanned skins using the solvent, perchloroethylene (PCE), in large dry-cleaning units. The use of this

solvent was coming under increasing environmental pressure: it seemed likely that PCE would become a 'black list' substance from the point of view of EC Directives, and, under the 1990 Environmental Protection Act, its use would entail regulation by Her Majesty's Inspectorate of Pollution (HMIP). To control emissions to atmosphere from the dry-cleaning units in line with EC legislation would have involved the installation of carbon recovery units at a cost of at least £25,000. Instead, the company decided to research an alternative method of extracting excess oil from the skins.

*The New Process*

After 12 months of experimentation with many different processes at pilot plant level, an effective system was identified. This could extract the excess oil to the required level using a water-based process. It was developed entirely in-house and worked without using any of the proprietary degreasing solutions which were beginning to appear on the market.

The unique process is critically dependent on keeping a large volume of water at a specific temperature within a narrow range of variation and maintaining precise pH control. The soap solution used has been specially formulated by the company and is biodegradable. The effluent is treated at the company's own effluent treatment plant before discharge.

Capital equipment costing £50,000 was needed for the new process. This included a stainless steel processing vessel, a hydraulic press to squeeze the liquor from the skins after degreasing, a new steam line, water pipework, pumps and electrical equipment. The old dry cleaning machines were converted in-house into tumble driers for the degreased skins. Including the research and development costs, the total cost of introducing the new process amounted to about £100,000.

The process has been an outstanding success. The company was the first chamois producer to stop using solvents for degreasing. As a result, it claims to be the only tannery in the UK which is not required to be regulated by HMIP. It is also saving on the costs of 10 tonnes of solvent per month, and as a result can produce chamois at a lower cost than its competitors. The lower boiling point of water compared to PCE has resulted in energy savings, and two large water coolers and a 35-tonne capacity tank for PCE have become redundant.

An important additional benefit is that, because the leathers produced using the new process are placed in water and not solvent, they are treated at a lower boiling point, and this produces chamois leathers with a 70% better water absorption capacity. The new chamois can now absorb up to seven times its own dry weight of water, exceeding the British Standard by a factor of almost two, thus making it an acknowledged world best for the removal of water.

The company has used the environmental and quality benefits of the new chamois to open up further business opportunities particularly in the USA and Europe. Sales to the USA were likely to at least double in 1993, and the company has gained the custom of a large Dutch retailer: in both cases as a direct result of the superior qualities, in both environmental and performance terms, of the new chamois.

### Example 13: British Steel Teesside Works, Redcar, Cleveland

*Background*

Teesside Works is one of the major operational sites of the Sections, Plates and Commercial Steels Business of British Steel. The main works site occupies an area of some 3000 acres, employs about 4500 people and produces up to 3.75 million tonnes of liquid steel per year.

The works produces sinter and coke for iron manufacture, makes iron in a blast furnace, and converts this into steel. The molten iron produced in the blast furnace is transported to the steel plant in large, rail-borne, refractory-lined steel vessels, known as torpedo ladles. These ladles have a capacity of 320 tonnes and transport the 94%-pure molten iron at a temperature of 1500°C.

The first operation at the steelmaking plant is to remove sulphur impurities from the iron in order to meet the specification for sulphur levels in the finished steel. Until 1992, this desulphurisation operation took place essentially in the open outside the main steelmaking plant. Calcium carbide was injected into the molten iron still in its torpedo ladle. A simple extractor hood over the torpedo ladle collected as much as possible of the fumes of iron oxide generated and emitted them via a stack without any cleaning. Not surprisingly, this operation was the subject of a large number of complaints from local members of the public and was the focus of regulatory pressures from the local Environmental Health Department and Her Majesty's Inspectorate of Pollution.

Following desulphurisation, the molten iron was then transferred into smaller iron transfer ladles and the slag produced as a result of the desulphurisation operation was skimmed off the top. Both these operations also produced iron oxide fume, but were carried out within the steelmaking building. The transfer operation was equipped with fume collection and cleaning facilities but the skimming operation was not. The fumes from this were not so visible, but affected the working environment inside the steelmaking building instead.

A new desulphurisation plant was needed, partly to address these environmental problems, but also because meeting the lower sulphur levels increasingly

required by customers with the existing plant resulted in other operational problems, both of which reduced the availability of the torpedo ladles:

- a deterioration in torpedo ladle refractory performance
- increasing problems filling the torpedo ladles because of excessive slag build up and skulling on the mouth of the ladle

*The New Desulphurisation Facility*

British Steel took the decision to opt for a state-of-the-art system which would meet not only current, but also likely future environmental regulatory requirements and which would enable them to achieve lower sulphur levels in their steel. All operations now take place within the steelmaking building. Molten iron is poured from the torpedo ladles into the transfer ladles before desulphurisation. These ladles are then moved to one of two desulphurisation stations. A lid containing the lance for injecting the desulphurising reagents in one half and a fume extraction system in the other half then closes over the top of the ladle. Desulphurisation is carried out using calcium carbide and magnesium transported to the injection lance under pressure in a so-called dense phase in a nitrogen atmosphere. The use of these two reagents in a dense phase is a novel technique developed in the USA.

The fume generated is extracted through the extractor hood to a new treatment system consisting of cyclones and a row of bag filters. The variable speed extractor fan is fitted with noise insulation. Slag generated in the desulphurisation process collects on the surface of the molten iron and is removed by drawing a rabbling arm over the surface of the molten metal. Finally, the lid covering the transfer ladle is opened and the ladle is moved to the next operation. The whole desulphurisation process is computer controlled and all the operations including the removal of slag can be carried out from a modern and pleasant control room. The entire operation takes place within the main steel conversion building and the new plant has also released an extraction fan which is now used to improve the removal of fume from other parts of the steelmaking operation.

Although the individual parts of the new system were not developed by British Steel, the complete system needed to be tailored to their specific requirements and represents a unique, state-of-the-art facility. Nevertheless, the project team, which involved both British Steel and Davy International (as the main contractor) were able to bring the project in on time and to budget.

The performance of the plant has exceeded expectations. With the old system, the weekly average net weight carried in the torpedo ladles was around 220 tonnes, mainly because of the constraints imposed by the use of the ladles in the desulphurisation operation. With the new facility, this weekly average almost immediately increased to 300 tonnes. The effective capacity of the ladle fleet has

been increased with associated benefits of reduced refractory costs, reduced iron losses, higher ladle availability and better scheduling, and fewer locomotive movements with a consequent fuel saving.

The new plant also enables the sulphur content of the iron to be much more closely controlled and is much more efficient in the use of reagents. Experience with the plant to date suggests that annual savings in the use of reagents alone will reach £1.3 million. The project was authorised on the basis that the £7.5 million investment would be recovered over 4.5 years; it is now thought that this sum will be recovered in 3 years.

The environmental performance of the plant is also better than expected. The fumes generated by the desulphurisation process are very evident on the video monitors on the plant, but there is no visible emission from the treatment plant stack. The visually intrusive emissions of brown iron oxide fume characteristic of the old plant have been eliminated and complaints from the public have ceased. The plant was designed to achieve a maximum dust emission of 30 $mg/m^3$ in order to meet not only the current requirement of 100 $mg/m^3$ but also the likely future requirement of 50 $mg/m^3$. In practice, the emissions from the treatment plant stack have not exceeded 10 $mg/m^3$.

### Example 14: J McIntyre (Non Ferrous) Ltd, Nottingham

*Background*

J McIntyre (Non Ferrous) Ltd is part of the Nottingham Metal Recyclers Group. It entered the aluminium scrap recycling business in the early 1970s when it took over the operation of a number of existing furnaces. Its final product is aluminium ingot of various types. By the late 1970s, the company's equipment was beginning to look outdated and inefficient, and the company therefore began to look for ways of increasing efficiency and reducing costs with new furnaces. In addition, the existing operations had all the pollution problems associated with secondary melting plants. The company was aware that any new plant would not be able to operate unless it was able to meet not only the current, but also future, pollution control regulations.

In order to be able to handle all types of incoming scrap aluminium, including, for example, soft drinks cans covered in paint and discarded aluminium window frames coated in plastic, the company had to operate seven different furnaces, and had to sort and pre-process its incoming material, depending on its degree of contamination, to take account of the different capabilities of the different furnaces. For practical reasons, therefore, the company wished to replace its seven units with one which would be capable of accepting any kind of scrap, clean or contaminated, thus saving on the need for sorting and pre-treatment. Priority was also given to finding a furnace technology able to meet all the

environmental regulations to the year 2000 and beyond. With the continuing deterioration in the quality of scrap and the increase in the amount of contamination it contained, this was becoming an increasingly stringent requirement.

The company set out to buy a furnace, and, over a seven year period, scoured the known world markets from Germany to Japan in the search for suitable equipment. The different types of furnace investigated included:

- **Reverbatory furnaces.** These are the most common types and are capable of melting large charges of clean mixed material. However, they cannot melt contaminated scrap material and pollution is difficult to control.

- **Rotary furnaces.** These are commonly used for melting aluminium scrap, especially the lighter, painted and contaminated material such as cans. Metal recovery rates are good but environmental performance is not. Salt fluxes are used to prevent oxidation, and these result in the need for costly fume filtration control to eliminate pollution to the atmosphere and a salt slab waste which requires special disposal.

- **Closed well furnaces.** These offer good metal recovery rates but suffer from slow melt rates and high energy costs per tonne of ingot. In addition, plastic coated metal (a form of scrap which is becoming more and more common) can sink into the well and give rise to rapid burning which causes excessive metal losses and increased dross formation.

- **Dry hearth furnaces.** These have always been the most universal type of furnace available for secondary aluminium melting. They can be charged with all types of aluminium scrap and any iron contamination dragged out via the front of the furnace. However, direct flame impingement can result in low metal recovery rates and high energy costs.

No unit on the market proved able to meet all McIntyre's requirements however, and in 1984 the company set out to design and build its own plant.

### *The New Furnace Design*

The need for an environmentally sound process was given a high priority in the design and because it led to the development of a completely sealed melting process (with neither smoke nor energy being emitted unnecessarily from any part of the plant) became the key to the unit's subsequent success. The design of the new plant is based around two furnaces. The first is a closed well furnace with a calculated slope to the furnace floor. This design dramatically improves heat transfer and reduces energy consumption. It also incorporates a hot gas recirculation system which is designed to ensure controlled burning of all

contaminated scrap before it sinks into the well of the furnace. This ensures that only clean, preheated, de-coated scrap enters the well, and thus results in a high metal recovery rate.

The second main furnace incorporated into the design is a dry hearth furnace. This has been completely redesigned and fitted with a hot gas recirculation system so that scrap can be de-coated by burning the organic components before the furnace burners come into operation. By melting this preheated scrap under a controlled flame, metal recovery rates are extremely high. On becoming molten, aluminium separates from any contaminants and runs to the back of the dry hearth chamber. Again the slope of the furnace floor has been carefully calculated and incorporates a holding bath. A certain amount of scrap can therefore be melted in the liquid bath rather than by direct flame, increasing metal recovery rates still further.

The need for a sealed system prompted one of the most important innovations on the plant: a unique and patented door sealing design which prevents emission of fumes and heat. This design is fitted to both the main furnaces. Finally, process control forms an essential part of the new system. This controls the return of the hot pyrolysis gas to the furnace system, and ensures that furnace pressures are kept uniform and that the unit is completely sealed. Process control also allows the operator to program the most efficient temperatures and melting times for different types of infeed material.

*Commercial and Environmental Benefits*

The new plant was finally completed in 1988. Its unique design results in increased metal recovery and a much lower energy use. It allows McIntyre (Non Ferrous) to process metal at about a third of the standard industrial cost. Any type of scrap can be charged into the plant without reduction in efficiency. For example, the furnace is now being used to melt light, thin-gauge material (the most difficult to deal with in terms of metal recovery and often uneconomical to process) without the use of salt fluxes, thus avoiding the need for costly fume filtration plant and salt disposal problems. The company can therefore afford to pay higher prices for its infeed material, encouraging the recycling of low grade material which would have been uneconomical to process.

As well as increasing energy efficiency, the concept of recirculation of gases also reduces environmental problems, since large volumes of air are not required to remove the contaminants. Only comparatively low-volume pollution control equipment is needed. Tests have so far shown that gases coming out of the plant are often cleaner than those going in, and the emission rates fall well within the most stringent environmental legislation.

Other benefits include a better working environment: there are fewer pollutants emitted into the work environment and no heat is emitted until the furnace doors are opened. This has resulted in reduced absenteeism and fewer worker illnesses. Downtime and breakdowns are also reduced because the furnace is process-controlled to a level which minimises wear and tear on parts. Finally, the quality of the final product is better and has BS5750 Stage 1 approval. As the product is also cheaper to produce, the company clearly has an edge over worldwide competition. In 1990, the new design won J McIntyre (Non Ferrous) Ltd the Queen's Award for Technology.

Although this had not been the original intention, McIntyre (Non Ferrous) has taken steps to market the new technology. Serious enquiries for the plant have been received from five multi-national companies for a total of 33 complete units.

## Chapter 9

## CONCLUSIONS

This report has provided a few examples of the business success which can result from a positive approach to environmental pressures. The examples reinforce the results of research which have shown that the companies most successful at managing environmental pressures are those which anticipate future legislative changes by:

- understanding the issues:
  - amongst environmental pressure groups
  - of concern to the public
  - for the regulator
  - of concern in other countries
- taking account of perceptions about issues as well the objective 'facts'.

It is particularly important to enter into dialogue with the various groups affected by the company's operations, including the local community, employees and pressure groups, and to understand their values and concerns.

The examples represent a wide range of industrial and commercial activities and describe companies from the small to the very large. Their experiences show clearly that waste is bad for business, and that good environmental management is one facet of good management. I hope these experiences will encourage many other companies to follow suit, to seize the opportunities on offer, and to win – the environmentally responsible way.

## FURTHER READING


Business in the Environment (1991) *Your Business and the Environment: An Executive Guide*, Business in the Environment, London, UK.

Confederation of British Industry/PA Consulting Group (1990) *Waking Up to a Better Environment: Results of a Survey on Attitudes Concerning the Environment*, CBI, London, UK.

PA Consulting Group (1990) *Profiting from the Environmental Challenge: Golden Leaf Awards 1990*, PA Consulting Group, Royston, UK.

PA Consulting Group (1991) *PA Golden Leaf Awards 1991 for Responsible Environmental Management*, PA Consulting Group, Royston, UK.

PA Consulting Group (1992) *PA Golden Leaf Awards 1992 for Responsible Environmental Management*, PA Consulting Group, Royston, UK.

Smith, D (1992) *Gaining a Clean Advantage: Creating Business Opportunity by Addressing Environmental Issues*, PA Consulting Group, Royston, UK.

Taylor, S (1992) Green Management: The Next Competitive Weapon. *Futures*, September, pp. 669-680.

3M United Kingdom plc (1990) *Integrating Environment into Business: A Guide to Policy Making and Implementation*, 3M United Kingdom plc.

Cairncross, F (1993) Waste and the Environment. *The Economist*, May 29th.

Department of Trade and Industry (1990) *Cutting Your Losses - A DTI Business Guide to Waste Minimisation*, DTI, London, UK.

Department of Trade and Industry (1992) *Cutting Your Losses 2: A Further Guide to Waste Minimisation for Business*, DTI, London, UK.

Department of the Environment (1990) *Clean Technology*, DoE, London, UK.

United Nations Environment Programme (1993) *Cleaner Production Worldwide*, UNEP Industry and Environment Programme Activity Centre, Paris, France.

British Telecommunications plc (1993) *BT and the Environment: Environmental Performance Report 1993*, BT, London, UK.

## USEFUL CONTACTS

The following names and telephone numbers have been taken from the Summer 1993 edition of the DTI's 'A Guide for Business':

**Department of Trade and Industry**
151 Buckingham Palace Road
London SW1W 9SS

| | | |
|---|---|---|
| Environmental Enquiry Point | Sue Plum | 0800 585 794 |
| Cleaner Technology and Waste Minimisation | Richard May | 071 215 1028 |
| BS7750 Environmental Management Systems Standard and Environmental Auditing | Peter Chandler | 071 215 1022 |
| Reclamation and Recycling | Mike Griffiths | 071 215 1036 |
| Waste Management | Barbara Langley | 071 215 1330 |

Other useful contacts include:

**Department of the Environment**
2 Marsham Street
London SW1P 3EB

| | | |
|---|---|---|
| Environmental Protection Technology | David Pounder | 071 276 3753 |

| | | |
|---|---|---|
| **The Conservation Foundation**<br>1 Kensington Gore<br>London SW7 2AR | David Shreeve | 071 823 8842 |